30 MUST-KNOW KEYS

TO

MASTERING SPOKEN ENGLISH

FROM LEARNER TO FLUENT SPEAKER

SHIVA PRASAD MILI

Notion Press India

Old No.38 New No.6
Mc Nichols Road, Chetpet
Chennai-600031

First Published by Notion Press 2023

First Edition: 2023

ISBN: 979-889233132-6

Printed and bound in India by Notion Press

30 MUST-KNOW KEYS

TO

MASTERING SPOKEN ENGLISH

(From Learner to Fluent Speaker)

Dear Reader,

In the cosmic library of choices, you unearth this book on **Mastering Spoken English**. Your selection isn't just a transaction; it's a shared journey towards eloquence. Each page becomes a step in this journey, coloured by your appreciation—an adventure we craft together.

Discovering fluency, one page at a time,

To your fluency,

Shiva Prasad Mili

Other Books by

<u>SHIVA PRASAD MILI</u>

1. Beliefs Across the River: Chronicles of the Mising Villages

2. Run-Movement for Drive and Purpose

3. Grammar Made Easy: Fluency Fix for English Learners

4. Essential Introduction to English Poetry: Comprehensive Guide for GEC Students

5. English Language Teaching: North East Perspectives (Edited 2014)

Dedication

This book is dedicated with warmth and gratitude to the spirited and diligent students of the Six-Month Certificate Course in Spoken English at Sibsagar Girls' College. Your commitment to mastering the art of spoken English has illuminated the classrooms and the path for others on this linguistic journey.

May the pages of this book serve as a companion in your ongoing pursuit of fluency, and may the confidence you gain in mastering spoken English echo in every conversation, story, and expression you share.

Acknowledgements

Within the pages of this book, gratitude unfolds like a captivating exploration intricately woven by the vibrant humanities enveloping me. Mentors, akin to guiding stars, illuminate the linguistic cosmos; students breathe life into the unfolding discourse. A special acknowledgement is reserved for the *participants* of the **Spoken English Course,** whose presence adds extraordinary brilliance to this evolving study. Friends, educators, and colleagues metamorphose the research process into a collaborative expedition.

A heartfelt note of gratitude is extended to **all** my English teachers for their indelible impact on my English study journey. It is imperative to express sincere appreciation to **Dr Z. N. Patil, Sawpon Dowerah,** and **Dr Protim Sharma,** revered figures in English language study in India. Their invaluable suggestions played a pivotal role in helping me **fine-tune** the book, refine its essence, and elevate its overall quality of expression.

As this academic journey takes centre stage, it carries the appreciation, sagacity, and collaborative spirit of a splendid community. Recognition is extended to all for being the indispensable threads in this compelling exploration.

Contents

SPECIAL MESSAGE FROM

-SCOTT GRANVILLE

With an insightful and comprehensive approach, Shiva Prasad Mili skilfully unpacks mastering the art of spoken communication, catering to both novices and aspiring fluent speakers. The author's passion for the subject is evident throughout the book, inspiring readers to embrace the challenges of the English language. This is an essential companion for anyone on the path to becoming a confident communicator in English.

His book is 'Unlocking Fluency: A Power-packed Guide for Beginners and Beyond."

Scott Granville

Co-Founder and Managing Director

Chasing Time English, NEW ZEALAND

Message and Praise for the book

'The book '30 Must-Know Keys to Mastering Spoken English: From Beginner to Fluent Speaker *is a must-have for anyone who desires to improve their fluency in spoken English. As non-native speakers of the English language, there are undoubtedly challenges to correctly communicating sounds and combinations of sounds in words. The author has diligently researched and identified the various problems. He has listed the essential 30 Must-know keys to help one manage and overcome these problems. I wish the author all the best in his endeavours.*

Prof (Dr) T K kharbamon
Vice-Chancellor, Martin Luther Christian University
&
**Former Director
English and Foreign Language University
Shillong, Nehu Campus**

Message and Praise for the book

'Delight courses through me as I share my enthusiasm for '30 Must-Know Keys to Mastering Spoken English' by Shiva Prasad Mili. This book will captivate undergraduates and postgraduates alike, offering a user-friendly exploration of vital oral communication skills in diverse real-life scenarios. Mili's dedication in crafting this invaluable manual is genuinely commendable.

I extend best wishes to Shiva Prasad Mili for providing a resource that is not only practical but also engaging. Particularly intriguing are his chapters on social expressions and fine-tuning, addressing essential aspects of alerting learners to potential pitfalls—an indispensable guide in developing practical communication skills. This work is more than a book; it is a compass steering English enthusiasts toward linguistic mastery.' I can say, ***This is one of the essential books to fine-tune your spoken English.***

Sawpon Dowerah

Former Academic Officer, Board of Secondary Education of Assam

&

Former Director, English Language Teaching Institute, Assam

Praise for the book

Communicative competence in English is more pronounced when it comes to spoken English, and the need for an easy-to-follow comprehensive guidebook in this regard has never lessened—'30 Must-know Keys to Master Spoken English, a skilfully designed self-learning book on spoken English in six parts. Starting with learning through listening, the mother language skill as the first key, the book presents the 30 key ideas, which include the basics of spoken English and a few advanced topics such as variety in expression and causative in the English language. As passionate and accomplished educator as he is, the writer Shiva Prasad Mili has done an excellent job writing this fine book for anyone interested in improving or fine-tuning their proficiency in spoken English.

Dr Protim Sharma

Writer and Columnist of 'Mind Your English'
The popular Language Column in
The Assam Tribune. (News Daily)

FOREWORD

It is said that there are four language skills: listening, speaking, reading, and writing. People perceive these skills from different orientations. Some people say that listening and reading are passive skills, and speaking and writing are active skills. This labelling stems from their perception of the organs involved. In their view, our ears and eyes do not take part actively like our organs of speech (lungs, windpipe, cavity of the mouth, cavity of the nose, the tongue, lips, and teeth) and organs of writing (the elbow, the forearm, the wrist, the palm, the fingers) do. This view is partially true. It is true that when we listen, our ears do not move, and when we read, our eyes move only a little. But we know that our ears receive spoken utterances and immediately pass them on to the brain for processing as our eyes catch written sentences and other visual symbols and forward them instantly to the brain for decoding. In this sense, listening and reading skills are as active as speaking and writing are. We can say that our ears and eyes are invisible participants in listening and reading. In speaking and writing, there are visible physical movements. Therefore, we can say that all four skills are active skills.

The order in which the four skills are traditionally mentioned or listed (listening, speaking, reading, and writing) does not represent reality. One can view these skills from two perspectives: from the input point of view and the output point of view. From the output point of view, the child first begins to listen and then begins to speak. In the same way, the child first begins to read and then begins to write. This legitimates the traditional order of skills (LSRW).

Logically speaking, someone has to say things first for me to hear them or listen to them. In other words, speaking precedes listening. By the same token, someone has to write something for me to read it. If there is no spoken output by a speaker, there is no spoken input for a listener. If there is no spoken output by a speaker, what do I listen to? Similarly, if there is no written output by a writer, there is no graphic input for me. I have nothing to read. This implies that writing precedes reading, doesn't it? So, the more logical sequence would be speaking followed by listening and writing followed by reading. Anyway, this is just an extra bit of information to adjust our attitudes.

Now, let me ask you an important question. Do you want to speak English confidently, fluently, appropriately, accurately, effectively, and efficiently? If you do, you need to master specific skills. Speaking isn't a single skill; it's a cluster of skills. Shiva Prasad Mili's book '30 **Must-Know Keys to Mastering Spoken English:** From Beginner to Fluent Speaker 'offers practical ways to develop your spoken English. I'd say that every teacher of English teaching spoken English at any level and every college and university library should have a copy of this book.

The book is a judicious blend of theoretical inputs and practical tips on Spoken English. If you follow the given instructions from cover to cover, you will undoubtedly become a competent speaker. **Good luck.**

Dr Z N Patil

Former **Professor of English**
&
Former Head, Department of Training and
Development,
**English and Foreign Languages University,
Hyderabad, India**

Preface

"The limits of my language mean the limits of my world."

--Ludwig Wittgenstein.

Welcome to the journey of mastering spoken English. This book, **"30 Must-Know Keys to Mastering Spoken English: From Learner to Fluent Speaker,"** is a culmination of years of experience, interactions, and the insights of students and language enthusiasts who, despite years of formal education, yearn to become confident/ fluent English speakers.

In the words of **George Bernard Shaw**, **"Language is the source of misunderstandings."** Rather than relying on narration of the contents, I have decided to give you the **keys** by which you can unlock the next step to *use and speak* up confidently. Each of the **30** keys is a practical tool to help you transform your knowledge into spoken fluency. From clear communication to active listening, politeness, and pronunciation, these keys will unlock your potential as a confident English speaker.

You are not alone on this journey. Many share their aspirations and challenges. With each key you master, you move closer to becoming the confident speaker you aspire to be.

The journey to becoming a confident speaker of the English language is a path often marked by uncertainty, hesitation, and frustration. Many of us have dedicated over a decade (**10 year**s) to learning English through academic settings. Yet, when it comes to real-world conversations, we may still find ourselves struggling to express our thoughts with fluency and confidence. The question that looms large is, "Why does this gap between knowledge and application persist?"

In crafting this book, I have listened closely to the stories of countless individuals grappling with this question. I have had the privilege of engaging with students and language enthusiasts who possess a wealth of knowledge about the English language, acquired through years of study, and yet remain apprehensive about speaking it. Their experiences have provided invaluable insights that underpin the essence of this book.

"30 Must-Know Keys to Mastering Spoken English" is *not just another language learning manual; it is a guiding light for those who have been on an extended journey with English but have not yet crossed the threshold of confident spoken communication*. It is designed to bridge the gap between academic learning and real-world application, offering practical, effective strategies that enable you to become a fluent and articulate speaker.

Each of the **30** keys presented within these pages draws upon the collective wisdom of language learners and educators, unveiling the hidden barriers that often hold us back from speaking confidently. These keys serve as your personalised toolkit, providing the essential skills, techniques, and strategies to unlock your full potential as a spoken English master.

But this book is not just about theory but about actionable steps. It is about the transformation that occurs when knowledge is converted into fluency and when hesitation gives way to confident expression. From the art of listening and speaking to the nuances of pronunciation, from understanding the cultural context of English to mastering everyday conversations, every key is a step toward breaking free from the shackles of **self-doubt and reluctance.**

So, let us begin this journey together, armed with the collective wisdom of those who have walked this path before us. Let us transform our knowledge into eloquence, hesitation into confidence, and dreams of English mastery into a living reality.

I firmly believe 'This is the book *you will ever need to meet the English challenge.'*

Author

Before you start:

In my interactions with English learners—students and educators alike—I've identified several key challenges:

1. **Lack of Confidence**: Many individuals struggle with expressing themselves due to a lack of confidence, fear of judgment, or mockery.

2. **Insufficient Practice:** A noticeable shortage of regular practice hinders the smooth application of learned concepts in real-life situations.

3. **Struggle with Word Choice**: Finding the right words poses a significant challenge, leading to frustration in accurately conveying thoughts.

4. **Correct Pronunciation Concerns**: Apprehension about making pronunciation mistakes and being laughed at adds to the complexity of the learning journey.

5. **Grammatical Insecurities:** Learners often feel insecure about grammatical errors, contributing to a sense of unease in communication.

This book with the **30** keys serves as a **comprehensive toolkit** to address these challenges. It offers guidance on confidence-building, effective practice, word choice, pronunciation, and grammatical correctness. This literary companion stands as a beacon, guiding learners towards becoming confident speakers who can navigate the complexities of English with ease.

Key 1

Listen and Learn

Ever wondered why listening takes the top spot in the language learning arena, especially when it comes to spoken English? Well, let me spill the beans – it's the unsung hero, the secret sauce, the golden key that opens the door to fluency. Here's the lowdown on why listening is your ticket to linguistic brilliance, aligning perfectly with the cornerstone of language skills - LSRW (Listening, Speaking, Reading, and Writing):

- *How you say it*: Listening can help you correctly say words. You can hear how native speakers stress some parts of the words, change their tone, and connect words. You can also learn how to say sounds that are not in your native language, like /th/ or /r/. By listening to different people, you can also learn how to change your way of speaking depending on who you are talking to and why.

- *What you say*: (Vocabulary): Listening can help you learn new words and phrases. You can hear how words are used in different situations and what they mean. You can also learn words that mean the same thing, words that mean the opposite thing, and words that go well together. By listening to different topics and types of texts, you can also learn words that are specific to certain fields and areas.

- *Why you say it*:(Grammar) Listening can help you learn the rules of grammar and how to use them. You can hear how native speakers use different structures and forms, and how they can change depending on the speaker, the listener, and the goal of the communication. You can also learn how to use words that show possibility, condition, action, and other things that can make your speech and writing more correct and powerful.

- *How well you say it*(Rhythm and Flow): Listening can help you speak more smoothly and confidently. You can hear how native speakers use words and sounds to fill the gaps, pause, and repeat when they speak. You can also learn how to use words and phrases that link your ideas and make them clear and logical.

Listening to English in various forms like podcasts, audiobooks, or movies is more than just absorbing information. It's an active engagement with culture and context. As we challenge ourselves with different levels of difficulty, we broaden our understanding, much like climbing a mountain. Each purpose of listening, whether for the main idea or details, hones unique comprehension skills. By listening often, we not only improve our English but also become better communicators and thinkers. So, let's truly listen, for our perception of the world lies in the words we hear.

Key 2

The English Alphabet

1. Building Blocks of Language:

- The English alphabet, with its 26 letters, is like a set of magical building blocks for words; each of these letters has a unique twin in upper and lower-case forms.

2. Alpha and Beta Beginnings:

- The name "alphabet" itself is a blend of "alpha" and "beta," the first two letters of the Greek alphabet, hinting at its historical roots.

3. Shaping Old English:

- Centuries ago, around the 7th century, the English alphabet was crafted to write Old English by borrowing from the Latin script, with letters being added and subtracted over time to shape the alphabet we know today.

History

4. Ancient Alphabetic Birth: - Alphabetic writing traces back around 4000 years. Imagine it as the dawn of a language's written journey.

5. Egyptian Beginnings:

 - Egypt, around 1800-1900 BC, played a significant role in the development of alphabetic writing, like the roots of a grand tree.

6. The Phoenician Bridge:

 - The Phoenicians built upon these early foundations, creating an alphabet that spread through the Mediterranean region like a summer breeze.

7. Greek Vowel :

 - The Greeks introduced vowels to the Phoenician resulting in what is known as the first true alphabet. It's like a symphony of language.

8. Roman Addition:

 - The Latins, or Romans, joined the chorus and added their touch. They mixed the Greek alphabet with Etruscan characters like 'S' and 'F' to shape the evolving script.

The British Transformation:

9. Roman Arrival in Britain:

 - When the Roman Empire set foot in Britain, they brought Latin. It was a historic encounter of cultures.

10. The Anglo-Saxon Angle:

   - In Britain, the Anglo-Saxons, a Germanic tribe, used Old English as their language, which was based on an older runic alphabet known as Futhorc.

11. The Alphabetic Blend:

   - The fusion of the Latin alphabet with Futhorc resulted in the modern English alphabet, like a recipe combining the finest ingredients.

Pronunciation Variation:

12. Z's Identity Shift:

   - It's intriguing to note that in both British and American English, most letters are pronounced the same way. However, 'Z' is a unique character. In British English, it's known as 'Zed,' while in American English, it goes by 'Zee.'

Pronunciation of the 26 Letters:

Let's start with the fun part – saying the letters out loud. It's like learning a new song!

1. **A** - It sounds like "ay," just like in "apple."

2. **B** - Say "bee," like the insect.

3. **C** - Pronounce it as "see."

4. **D** - It's "dee," like in "dog."

5. **E** - It sounds like "ee," as in "elephant."

6. **F** - Say "eff," just like "football."

7. **G** - "Jee" is the sound, like in "giraffe."

8. **H** - It's "aych," as in "house."

9. **I** - Say "eye," like the one you see with.

10. **J** - "Jay," like "jump."

11. **K** - It's "kay," just like "kite."

12. **L** - Say "el," like in "lion."

13. **M** - It's "em," just like "monkey."

14. **N** - "En" is the sound, like in "nose."

15. **O** - Say "oh," like "octopus."

16. **P** - Pronounce it as "pee," as in "panda."

17. **Q** - "Kyoo" is the sound, like "queen."

18. **R** - It sounds like "ar," just like "rabbit."

19. **S** - Say "ess," like "snake."

20. **T** - "Tee," just like "turtle."

21. **U** - It's "you," as in "unicorn."

22. **V** - Pronounce it as "vee," like "volcano."

23. *W* - "Double you" because it looks like two "U"s joined.

24. **X** - "Eks," like "xylophone."

25. **Y** - It sounds like "why," like asking a question.

26. **Z** - "Zee," just like "zebra."

Here is the list of the 26 English letters with their pronunciation in the International Phonetic Alphabet (IPA):

English Alphabet	IPA Pronunciation	Hindi Pronunciation
A	/eɪ/	ए
B	/biː/	बी
C	/siː/	सी
D	/diː/	डी
E	/iː/	ई
F	/ɛf/	एफ
G	/dʒiː/	जी
H	/eɪtʃ/	एच

English Alphabet	IPA Pronunciation	Hindi Pronunciation
I	/aɪ/	आई
J	/dʒeɪ/	जे
K	/keɪ/	के
L	/ɛl/	एल
M	/ɛm/	एम
N	/ɛn/	एन
O	/oʊ/	ओ
P	/piː/	पी
Q	/kjuː/	क्यू

English Alphabet	IPA Pronunciation	Hindi Pronunciation
R	/ɑːr/	आर
S	/ɛs/	एस
T	/tiː/	टी
U	/juː/	यू
V	/viː/	वी
W	/ˈdʌbljuː/	डब्लू
X	/ɛks/	एक्स
Y	/waɪ/	वाई
Z	/zɛd/	जेड

Key 3

English Pronunciation

(A)

English Letters and Sounds: Their Correspondence

English is not a **phonetic** language, which means that the way we **write** words and the way we **say** them are not always the same. There are many reasons for this, such as the **history** of the language, the **influence** of other languages, and the **changes** in pronunciation over time. Let me explain some of the differences between **letters** and **sounds** in English.

• **Letters** are the written symbols that we use to represent the sounds of the language. They are also called **graphemes**. There are 26 letters in the English alphabet, but they can be combined in different ways to make more sounds.

- **Sounds** are the units of speech that we produce with our vocal organs, such as our lips, tongue, and voice box. They are also called **phonemes**. There are about 44 sounds in spoken English, but the number can vary depending on the **accent** or **dialect** of the speaker.

- Sometimes one letter can make more than one sound. For example, the letter "a" can make different sounds in words like "cat", "cake", "car", and "all". • Sometimes one sound can be written with more than one letter. For example, the sound /k/ can be written with "c", "k", "ck", or "ch" in words like "cat", "king", "duck", and "school".

- Sometimes the same combination of letters can make different sounds. For example, the letters "ough" can make different sounds in words like "though", "through", "cough", "rough", "plough", "ought", and "borough".

- Sometimes some letters are not pronounced at all. For example, the letter "k" is silent in words like "know", "knife", and "knock".

- Consider the letter 'C.' It can represent the /k/ sound in words like "cat" or the /s/ sound in words like "city." The letter 'S' can be pronounced as /s/ in "see" or as /z/ in "rose." This variability is what makes English pronunciation notoriously tricky.

These differences can make English spelling and pronunciation challenging for learners, but they also provide clues about the **origin**, **meaning**, and **history** of words. For example, words that end with "-tion" are usually from Latin, and words that start with "kn-" are usually from Germanic languages

(B)

20 Vowels and 24 Consonants

English pronunciation is the way we say the words of the English language. It is important for spoken English because it helps us ***communicate clearly and effectively with other people.*** If we pronounce words correctly, we can avoid misunderstandings and confusion. If we pronounce words incorrectly, ***we can cause problems and embarrassment***. For example, if we say, "**I want a sheet of paper**" but we pronounce "**sheet" as "shit**", we can offend someone or make them laugh. If we say **"I like your accent"** but we pronounce **"accent"** as **"assent"**, we ***can confuse someone or make them think we agree with them.***

To **improve our English pronunciation**, we need to learn the sounds of the language and how they are represented by letters or symbols. There are **20 vow**el sounds and **24 consonant** sounds in English. Each sound has a symbol in the **International Phonetic Alphabet** (IPA), which is a system of writing down how words are pronounced. The IPA symbols can help us learn how to say words correctly because they show us the exact sounds and not the spelling. For example, the word "cat" has an IPA transcription of /kæt/, which tells us how to pronounce each sound in the word.

We also need to practise our English pronunciation by listening to native speakers and imitating their speech. We can use various resources to help us with this, such as online dictionaries, podcasts, videos, songs, and apps. We can also ask for feedback from teachers, friends, or online tutors. By practising our English pronunciation regularly, we can improve our spoken English skills and confidence.

Here is a list of 20 English vowel Sounds:

Vowel Phonemes	Example Words

Pure Vowel Sounds:

1. **/iː/**
   - **Hindi Counterpart:**ई (ee) as in ईंट (eent - brick)
   - **Key Word:** "See"
2. **/ɪ/**
   - **Hindi Counterpart:**इ (i) as in बिल्ली (billi - cat)
   - **Key Word:** "Sit"
3. **/e/**
   - **Hindi Counterpart:**ए (e) as in खेल (khel - play)
   - **Key Word:** "Dress"
4. **/æ/**
   - **Hindi Counterpart:**ऐ (ai) as in ऐनक (ainak - glasses)
   - **Key Word:** "Cat"

5. **/ɑː/**

- - **Hindi Counterpart:**आ （aa) as in आम（aam - mango)
  - **Key Word:** "Car"

6. **/ɒ/**
   - - **Hindi Counterpart:**ऑ （o) as in ऑटो（auto - auto)
     - **Key Word:** "Dog"

7. **/ʌ/**
   - - **Hindi Counterpart:**अ （a) as in अगर（agar - if)
     - **Key Word:** "Cup"

8. **/ʊ/**
   - - **Hindi Counterpart:**उ （u) as in उल्लू（ullu - owl)
     - **Key Word:** "Book"

9. **/u:/**
   - - **Hindi Counterpart:**ऊ （oo) as in ऊँट（unt - camel)
     - **Key Word:** "True"

10. **/ɜ:/**
    - - **Hindi Counterpart:**अर （ar) as in अरे（are - hey)
      - **Key Word:** "Herb"

11. **/ə/**
    - - **Hindi Counterpart:**अ （a) as in अगर（agar - if)
      - **Key Word:** "Sofa"

12. **/ɔ:/**
    - - **Hindi Counterpart:**ओ （o) as in ओर（aur - and)
      - **Key Word:** "Thought"

Diphthongs⊗ (Vowel Glide)

1. **/aɪ/**
   - **Hindi Counterpart:**आई （aai) as in आई （aai - came)
   - **Key Word:** "Price"

2. **/aʊ/**
   - **Hindi Counterpart:**आऊ （aau) as in आऊँगा （aaunga - will come)
   - **Key Word:** "Out"

3. **/ɪə/**
   - **Hindi Counterpart:**इअ （ia) as in इअर （iar - ear)
   - **Key Word:** "Here"

4. **/eə/**
   - **Hindi Counterpart:**एअ （ea) as in एअर （ear - air)
   - **Key Word:** "Air"

5. **/ʊə/**
   - **Hindi Counterpart:**उअ （ua) as in उअर （uar - war)
   - **Key Word:** "Tour"

6. **/ɔɪ/**
   - **Hindi Counterpart:**ओई （oi) as in ओई （oi - hey)
   - **Key Word:** "Coin"

7. **/eɪ/**
   - **Hindi Counterpart:**ए （e) as in खेल （khel - play)
   - **Key Word:** "Face"

8. **/əʊ/**

- o **Hindi Counterpart:**ओ (o) as in ओर (aur - and)
- o **Key Word:** "Go"

This makes a total of 20 vowel sounds (12 pure vowels + 8 diphthongs). Please note that these are general pronunciations and can vary based on accent and regional dialects. For a more comprehensive list and practising pronunciation, you might find online resources like [toPhonetics] and [English Reservoir] helpful. They provide audio and video recordings of native speakers, which can be very useful for improving pronunciation.

Hindi and Assamese Counterparts for the 24 RP consonant sounds.

Stops:
1. **/p/**
   - **Hindi Counterpart:**प (pa)
   - **Assamese Counterpart:**প (po)
   - **Key Word:** "Pot"
2. **/b/**
   - **Hindi Counterpart:**ब (ba)
   - **Assamese Counterpart:**ব (bo)
   - **Key Word:** "Bat"
3. **/t/**
   - **Hindi Counterpart:**त (ta)
   - **Assamese Counterpart:**ট (to)
   - **Key Word:** "Top"
4. **/d/**
   - **Hindi Counterpart:**ड (da)

- **Assamese Counterpart:**ড
- **Key Word:** "Dog"

5. **/k/**
  - **Hindi Counterpart:**क (ka)
  - **Assamese Counterpart:**ক (ko)
  - **Key Word:** "Cat"

6. **/g/**
  - **Hindi Counterpart:**ग (ga)
  - **Assamese Counterpart:**গ (go)
  - **Key Word:** "Go"

Fricatives:
7. **/f/**
  - **Hindi Counterpart:**फ (pha)
  - **Assamese Counterpart:**ফ (fo)
  - **Key Word:** "Fish"

8. **/v/**
  - **Hindi Counterpart:**व (va)
  - **Assamese Counterpart:**ভ (bho)
  - **Key Word:** "Van"

9. **/θ/**
  - **Hindi Counterpart:**थ (tha)
  - **Assamese Counterpart:**থ (tho)
  - **Key Word:** "Thin"

10. **/ð/**
  - **Hindi Counterpart:**द (da)
  - **Assamese Counterpart:**দ (do)
  - **Key Word:** "This"

11. **/s/**
  - **Hindi Counterpart:**स (sa)
  - **Assamese Counterpart:**চ (so)
  - **Key Word:** "Sun"

12. **/z/**
  - **Hindi Counterpart:**ज़ (za)

- **Assamese Counterpart:**জ (zo)
- **Key Word:** "Zip"

13. **/ʃ/**

- **Hindi Counterpart:**श (sha)
- **Assamese Counterpart:**শ (xo)
- **Key Word:** "Shoe"

14. **/ʒ/**

- **Hindi Counterpart:**ज (zha)
- **Assamese Counterpart:**ঝ (jho)
- **Key Word:** "Measure"

Affricates:

15. **/tʃ/**

- **Hindi Counterpart:**च (cha)
- **Assamese Counterpart:**চ (cho)
- **Key Word:** "Chat"

16. **/dʒ/**

- **Hindi Counterpart:**ज (ja)
- **Assamese Counterpart:**জ (zo)
- **Key Word:** "Judge"

Nasals:

17. **/m/**

- **Hindi Counterpart:**म (ma)
- **Assamese Counterpart:**ম (mo)
- **Key Word:** "Mat"

18. **/n/**

- **Hindi Counterpart:**न (na)
- **Assamese Counterpart:**ন (no)
- **Key Word:** "Net"

19. **/ŋ/**

- **Hindi Counterpart:**ङ
- **Assamese Counterpart:**ঙ (ngo)
- **Key Word:** "Sing"

Liquids:

20. **/l/**
- **Hindi Counterpart:**ल (la)
- **Assamese Counterpart:**ল (lo)
- **Key Word:** "Lip"

21. **/r/**
- **Hindi Counterpart:**र (ra)
- **Assamese Counterpart:**ৰ (ro)
- **Key Word:** "Run"

Semivowels:

22. **/w/**
- **Hindi Counterpart:**व (va)
- **Assamese Counterpart:**ৱ (wo)
- **Key Word:** "Wet"

23. **/j/**
- **Hindi Counterpart:**य (ya)
- **Assamese Counterpart:**য (yo)
- **Key Word:** "Yes"

Glides:

24. **/h/**
- **Hindi Counterpart:**ह (ha)
- **Assamese Counterpart:**হ (ho)
- **Key Word:** "Hat"

This comprehensive overview now includes both Hindi and Assamese counterparts, providing a richer understanding of the diverse phonetic expressions across these languages.

Takeaways

1. English pronunciation is essential for effective communication.

2. Accurate pronunciation ensures clarity and reduces misunderstanding.

3. Good pronunciation contributes to fluency and confidence.

4. Confidence in spoken English is boosted by accurate pronunciation.

5. Proficient pronunciation enhances listening and comprehension.

(c)

Now let me introduce you to the following:

Do you want to learn how to say and pronounce the **7 days of the week**, **12 months in a year** and the **4 seasons** in English? Do you want to know how to write the sounds of these words using symbols? If yes, then you need to learn about phonetic transcription in English.

Phonetic transcription is a way of writing the sounds of a language using special symbols. These symbols are called the International Phonetic Alphabet (IPA). The IPA has a symbol for every sound in any language. For example, the symbol /a/ represents the sound in the word "cat".

Phonetic transcription can help you learn how to pronounce English words correctly. It can also help you understand the differences between British and American pronunciation. For example, the word "water" is pronounced differently in British and American English. In phonetic transcription, we can write it as /ˈwɔːtə/ in British English and /ˈwɑːtər/ in American English.

Let's see how we can use phonetic transcription to write and say the 7 days of the week, 12 months in a year and the four seasons in English.

Days of the week

Here are the 7 days of the week in English with their phonetic transcription and pronunciation:

- **Monday - /ˈmʌndeɪ/ - MUN-day**
- **Tuesday - /ˈtjuːzdeɪ/ - TYOOZ-day**
- **Wednesday - /ˈwenzdeɪ/ - WENZ-day**
- **Thursday - /ˈθɜːzdeɪ/ - THURZ-day**
- **Friday - /ˈfraɪdeɪ/ - FRY-day**
- **Saturday - /ˈsætədeɪ/ - SAT-uh-day**
- **Sunday - /ˈsʌndeɪ/ - SUN-day**

Some tips to remember:

- The first syllable of each day is stressed, which means it is louder and longer than the other syllables.

- The letter "d" in the second syllable is pronounced like a soft "t" in American English but like a hard "d" in British English.

- The letter "s" in Saturday is pronounced like a "z" in both British and American English.

Months of the year

Here are the 12 months of the year in English with their phonetic transcription and pronunciation:

- **January - /ˈdʒænjuəri/ - JAN-yoo-uh-ree**

- **February - /ˈfebruəri/ - FEB-roo-uh-ree**

- **March - /mɑːrtʃ/ - MAARCH**

- **April - /ˈeɪprəl/ - AY-pruhl**

- **May - /meɪ/ - MAY**

- **June - /dʒuːn/ - JOON**

- **July - /dʒuˈlaɪ/ - joo-LIE**

- **August - /ˈɔːgəst/ - AW-guhst**

- **September - /sepˈtembər/ - sep-TEM-bur**

- **October - /ɒkˈtəʊbər/ - ok-TOH-bur**

- **November - /nəʊˈvembər/ - noh-VEM-bur**

- **December - /dɪˈsembər/ - di-SEM-bur**

Some tips to remember:

- The first syllable of each month is stressed, except for July, which has the stress on the second syllable.

- The letter "r" at the end of the word is pronounced in American English, but not in British English.

- The letter "u" in August is pronounced like an "aw" sound in both British and American English.

Seasons of the year

Here are the 4 seasons of the year in English with their phonetic transcription and pronunciation:

- **Spring - /sprɪŋ/ - SPRING**

- **Summer - /ˈsʌmər/ - SUM-ur**

- **Autumn - /ˈɔːtəm/ - AW-tum**

- **Winter - /ˈwɪntər/ - WIN-tur**

Some tips to remember:

- The first syllable of each season is stressed, except for Autumn, which has the stress on both syllables.

- The letter "g" in Spring is pronounced like a "ng" sound in both British and American English.

- The word Autumn is also called Fall in American English, which is pronounced /fɔːl/ - FAWL.

The 7 days of the week, 12 months in a year and the four seasons are very important words in English because they are a part of our life and day-to-day experiences. We use them to talk about many things, such **as our schedule, our plans, our events, our memories, our birthdays, our holidays, our seasons, our festivals, our weather, our activities, our clothes, and our moods. For example, we can say:**

- I have a meeting on Monday and I am going to the cinema on Friday.

- I was born in June and I celebrate Diwali in November.

- I like spring because it is warm and sunny, but I hate winter because it is cold and dark.

Can we have the pronunciation of commonly used words:

Cardinal Numbers (1-50):

1. **One (1):** /wʌn/

2. **Two (2):** /tuː/

3. **Three (3):** /θriː/

4. **Four (4):** /fɔː/

5. **Five (5):** /faɪv/

6. **Six (6):** /sɪks/

7. **Seven (7):** /ˈsɛv.ən/

8. **Eight (8):** /eɪt/

9. **Nine (9):** /naɪn/

10. **Ten (10):** /tɛn/

11. **Eleven (11):** /ɪˈlɛv.ən/

12. **Twelve (12):** /twɛlv/

13. **Thirteen (13):** /ˌθɜːˈtiːn/

14. **Fourteen (14):** /ˌfɔːˈtiːn/

15. **Fifteen (15):** /ˌfɪfˈtiːn/

16. **Sixteen (16):** /sɪksˈtiːn/

17. **Seventeen (17):** /ˌsɛv.ənˈtiːn/

18. **Eighteen (18):** /ɪˈteɪnˈtiːn/

19. **Nineteen (19):** /ˌnaɪnˈtiːn/

20. **Twenty (20):** /ˈtwɛn.ti/

21. **Twenty-one (21):** /ˈtwɛn.tiˈwʌn/

22. **Twenty-two (22):** /ˈtwɛn.tituː/

23. **Twenty-three (23):** /ˈtwɛn.tiθriː/

24. **Twenty-four (24):** /ˈtwɛn.tifɔː/

25. **Twenty-five (25):** /ˈtwɛn.tifaɪv/

26. **Twenty-six (26):** /ˈtwɛn.tisɪks/

27. **Twenty-seven (27):** /ˈtwɛn.tiˈsɛv.ən/

28. **Twenty-eight (28):** /ˈtwɛn.tieɪt/

29. **Twenty-nine (29):** /ˈtwɛn.tinaɪn/

30. **Thirty (30):** /ˈθɜː.ti/

31. **Thirty-one (31):** /ˈθɜː.tiwʌn/

32. **Thirty-two (32):** /ˈθɜː.tituː/

33. **Thirty-three (33):** /ˈθɜː.tiθriː/

34. **Thirty-four (34):** /ˈθɜː.tifɔː/

35. **Thirty-five (35):** /ˈθɜː.tifaɪv/

36. **Thirty-six (36):** /ˈθɜː.ti.sɪks/

37. **Thirty-seven (37):** /ˈθɜː.tiˈsɛv.ən/

38. **Thirty-eight (38):** /ˈθɜː.tieɪt/

39. **Thirty-nine (39):** /ˈθɜː.tinaɪn/

40. **Forty (40):** /ˈfɔː.ti/

41. **Forty-one (41):** /ˈfɔː.tiwʌn/

42. **Forty-two (42):** /ˈfɔː.tituː/

43. **Forty-three (43):** /ˈfɔː.tiθriː/

44. **Forty-four (44):** /ˈfɔː.tifɔː/

45. **Forty-five (45):** /ˈfɔː.tifaɪv/

46. **Forty-six (46):** /ˈfɔː.tisɪks/

47. **Forty-seven (47):** /ˈfɔː.tiˈsɛv.ən/

48. **Forty-eight (48):** /ˈfɔː.tieɪt/

49. **Forty-nine (49):** /ˈfɔː.tinaɪn/

50. **Fifty (50):** /ˈfɪf.ti/

Ordinal Numbers (1-10):

1. **First (1st):** /fɜːst/

2. **Second (2nd):** /ˈsɛk.ənd/

3. **Third (3rd):** /θɜːd/

4. **Fourth (4th):** /fɔːθ/

5. **Fifth (5th):** /fɪfθ/

6. **Sixth (6th):** /sɪksθ/

7. **Seventh (7th):** /ˈsɛv.ənθ/

8. **Eighth (8th):** /eɪtθ/

9. **Ninth (9th):** /naɪnθ/

10. **Tenth (10th):** /tɛnθ/

Numerals of Frequency:

1. **Once:** /wʌns/

2. **Twice:** /twaɪs/

3. **Thrice:** /θraɪs/

4. **Four times:** /fɔːrtaɪmz/

5. **Five times:** /faɪvtaɪmz/

6. **Six times:** /sɪkstaɪmz/

7. **Seven times:** /ˈsɛv.əntaɪmz/

8. **Eight times:** /eɪttaɪmz/

9. **Nine times:** /naɪntaɪmz/

10. **Ten times:** /tɛntaɪmz/

50 Daily Commonly Used Words with IPA:

1. **Hello:** /həˈləʊ/

2. **Goodbye:** /gʊdˈbaɪ/

3. **Please:** /pliːz/

4. **Thank You:** /ˌθæŋkjʊ/

5. **Sorry:** /ˈsɒri/

6. **Yes:** /jes/

7. **No:** /nəʊ/

8. **Excuse me:** /ɪkˈskjuːz miː/

9. **What's your name?:** /wɒtsjʊərneɪm/

10. **How are you?:** /haʊərjuː/

11. **I love you:** /aɪlʌvjʊ/

12. **What time is it?:** /wɒttaɪmɪzɪt/

13. **Where is the nearest...?:** /wɛərɪzðəˈnɪərɪst/

14. **Nice to meet you:** /naɪstʊmiːtjʊ/

15. **Okay:** /əʊˈkeɪ/

16. **Sorry,I don't understand:** /ˈsɒri aɪ doʊnt ˌʌndəˈstænd/

17. **Sure:** /ʃʊər/

18. **See you later:** /sijʊˈleɪtər/

19. **Bye:** /baɪ/

20. **Good morning:** /gʊdˈmɔːrnɪŋ/

21. **Good night:** /gʊdnaɪt/

22. **How's it going?:** /haʊzɪtˈgoʊɪŋ/

23. **Fine:** /faɪn/

24. **Great:** /greɪt/

25. **Yes, please:** /jespliːz/

26. **No, thank you:** /nəʊθæŋkjʊ/

27. **Can I help you?:** /kænaɪˈhɛlpjʊ/

28. **What's up?:** /wɒtsʌp/

29. **I'm sorry:** /aɪmˈsɒri/

30. **You're welcome:** /jʊrˈwɛlkəm/

31. **How was your day?:** /haʊwəzjʊrdeɪ/

32. **I don't know:** /aɪdoʊntnoʊ/

33. **Let's go:** /lɛtsgoʊ/

34. **How much is it?:** /haʊmʌʧɪzɪt/

35. **Where are you from?:** /wɛrərjʊfrʌm/

36. **What's the weather like?:** /wɒtsðəˈwɛðərlaɪk/

37. **I'm fine, thank you:** /aɪmfaɪnθæŋkjʊ/

38. **Could you repeat that?:** /kʊdjʊrɪˈpiːtðæt/

39. **I need help:** /aɪnidhɛlp/

40. **How do you do?:** /haʊdʊjʊ duː/

41. **That's great:** /ðætsgreɪt/

42. **I'm here:** /aɪmhɪər/

43. **Do you understand?:** /du jʊˌʌndərˈstænd/

44. **Sorry to bother you:** /ˈsɒrɪtʊˈbɒðərjʊ/

45. **Let me think:** /lɛtmiːθɪŋk/

46. **I don't think so:** /aɪdoʊntθɪŋksoʊ/

47. **What's the plan?:** /wɒtsðəplæn/

48. **Where's the bathroom?:** /wɛrzðəˈbæθrʊm/

49. **Nice weather today:** /naɪsˈwɛðərtəˈdeɪ/

50. **It's beautiful:** /ɪtsˈbjuːtɪfəl/

<u>50 Family-Related Words with IPA</u>

1. **Father:** /ˈfɑːðə/

2. **Mother:** /ˈmʌðə/

3. **Daughter:** /ˈdɔːtə/

4. **Son:** /sʌn/

5. **Sister:** /ˈsɪstə/

6. **Brother:** /ˈbrʌðə/

7. **Cousin:** /ˈkʌzən/

8. **Aunt:** /ænt/

9. **Uncle:** /ˈʌŋkəl/

10. **Grandmother:** /ˈgrændˌmʌðə/

11. **Grandfather:** /ˈgrændˌfɑːðə/

12. **Niece:** /niːs/

13. **Nephew:** /ˈnɛfjuː/

14. **Husband:** /ˈhʌzbənd/

15. **Wife:** /waɪf/

16. **Parents:** /ˈpɛrənts/

17. **Children:** /ˈtʃɪldrən/

18. **In-laws:** /ɪnlɔːz/

19. **Spouse:** /spaʊs/

20. **Family:** /ˈfæməli/

21. **Kin:** /kɪn/

22. **Siblings:** /ˈsɪblɪŋz/

23. **Maternal:** /məˈtɜːrnəl/

24. **Paternal:** /pəˈtɜːrnəl/

25. **Twin:** /twɪn/

26. **Stepmother:** /stɛpˈmʌðər/

27. **Stepfather:** /stɛpˈfɑːðər/

28. **Half-sister:** /hæfˈsɪstər/

29. **Half-brother:** /hæfˈbrʌðər/

30. **Nuclear family:** /ˈnjuːklɪərˈfæməli/

31. **Extended family:** /ɪkˈstɛndɪdˈfæməli/

32. **Adoptive parents:** /əˈdɒptɪvˈpɛrənts/

33. **Orphan:** /ˈɔːrfən/

34. **Custody:** /ˈkʌstədi/

35. **Lineage:** /ˈlɪniːɪdʒ/

36. **Descendant:** /dɪˈsɛndənt/

37. **Ancestor:** /ˈænsɛstər/

38. **Godparent:** /ˈgɒdˌpɛrənt/

39. **Godchild:** /ˈgɒdˌtʃaɪld/

40. **Foster family:** /ˈfɒstərˈfæməli/

41. **Inheritance:** /ɪnˈhɛrɪtəns/

42. **Heritage:** /ˈhɛrɪtɪdʒ/

43. **Alimony:** /ˈælɪməni/

44. **Spousal support:** /ˈspaʊzəlsəˈpɔːrt/

45. **Joint custody:** /dʒɔɪntˈkʌstədi/

46. **Sibling rivalry:** /ˈsɪblɪŋˈraɪvəlri/

47. **Kith and kin:** /kɪθəndkɪn/

48. **Fraternal twins:** /ˈfrætərnəltwɪnz/

49. **Maternal instinct:** /məˈtɜːrnəlˈɪnstɪŋkt/

50. **Generations:** /ˌdʒɛnəˈreɪʃənz/

The International Phonetic Alphabet (IPA) symbols provided here aim to capture the nuances of English pronunciation, allowing for a more comprehensive understanding of the spoken

If we pronounce these words correctly, we can make our spoken English sound better and more enticing.

Let's use this gap:

The everyday lexicon that accompanies us from the morning's first light to the evening's gentle dusk. Each word, an indispensable companion in the symphony of daily life, is adorned with its unique International Phonetic Alphabet (IPA) pronunciation, creating a melodic harmony of sounds.

1. **Wake up** /weɪk ʌp/
2. **Toothbrush** /tuːθbrʌʃ/
3. **Breakfast** /ˈbrɛkfəst/
4. **Commute** /kəˈmjuːt/
5. **Coffee** /ˈkɒfi/
6. **Deadline** /ˈdɛdlaɪn/
7. **Lunchtime** /ˈlʌntaɪm/
8. **Email** /ˈiːmeɪl/
9. **Meeting** /ˈmiːtɪŋ/
10. **Afternoon** /ˌæftəˈnuːn/
11. **Productivity** /ˌprɒdʌkˈtɪvɪti/
12. **Traffic** /ˈtræfɪk/
13. **Dinner** /ˈdɪnər/
14. **Exercise** /ˈɛksəsaɪz/
15. **Conversation** /ˌkɒnvəˈseɪʃən/
16. **Relaxation** /ˌriːlækˈseɪʃən/
17. **Chores** /ʧɔːz

Key 4

Learning Phrases not only Words

Learning a New Language: It's More Than Just Words

You have been learning English for more than 10+2+3+2 years right? What have you been doing? You have been **memorising words, drilling grammar rules, and maybe even trying to perfect your accent.** But have you ever stopped to think about **phrases?**

Learning a new language is not just about memorizing words and grammar rules. It's also about understanding how words are used together to form meaningful and natural expressions. These expressions are called phrases, and they are the building blocks of spoken language. Phrases are groups of words that naturally fit together in a language, such as "Nice to meet you", "how are you doing?", or "what are you up to?".

The Hidden Power of Phrases

Let's think about this for a moment. If you're learning to play a musical instrument, you don't just learn the notes, right? You learn chords, scales, and how to put those notes together to make music. Similarly, when you're learning English, knowing individual words is like knowing the notes. But to make music, or in this case, to speak fluently, you need to learn phrases.

Phrases are like the **secret sauce** of any language. They're groups of words that work together to convey a particular meaning. For example, **'break a leg'** doesn't literally mean to break your leg. It's a phrase used to wish someone good luck!

Why Learning Phrases is Better Than Learning Isolated Words

Learning phrases is better than learning isolated words for several reasons:

1. Phrases help you to sound more natural and native-like. When you learn phrases, you learn how words are actually used in real-life situations, not just in dictionaries or textbooks. You learn the **common collocations, idioms, and slang** that native speakers use every day. Native speakers use phrases all the time without even realizing it. For example, instead of learning the word **"breakfast" alone, you can learn the phrase "have breakfast" or "make breakfast",** which are more natural and common ways to use the word. Learning phrases can also help you **avoid errors** or **awkward language** that may **confuse or distract your listener**. For example, in English, you say "strong wind" but "heavy rain". It would not be normal to say "heavy wind" or "strong rain".

2. Phrases help you to speak more fluently and confidently. When you learn phrases, you learn chunks of language that you can use as they are, without having to think too much about grammar or word order. Instead of struggling to put together a sentence word by word, you can use a phrase to express a complex idea quickly. It's like having a shortcut!

Phrases can help you to speak faster and more smoothly and reduce the number of pauses and hesitations in your speech. Learning phrases can also help you to overcome the fear of speaking, as you can rely on the phrases that you have learned to start and maintain a conversation, even if you don't know every word or rule in the language.

3. Phrases help you to understand spoken language better. When you learn phrases, you learn to recognize and process familiar word combinations more easily than unfamiliar ones. This can help you to understand spoken language faster and more accurately, as you can catch the meaning and intention of the speaker more quickly. Learning phrases can also help you to cope with different accents, dialects, and speeds of speech, as you can focus on the phrases that you have learned rather than on every single word or sound.

How to Use Phrases Effectively as a Mastery Key for Mastering Spoken Language

To use phrases effectively as a mastery key for mastering spoken language, you need to learn them and practice them. Here are some tips and strategies that can help you:

- **Use a good dictionary or a phrase list to look up the words that form phrases with the word you want to use.** For example, you can use the [Oxford Collocations Dictionary] or the [Cambridge English Collocations in Use books] to find out the common phrases for different words. These resources can also provide examples of how to use the phrases in sentences.
- **Pay attention to the phrases that you hear or read in natural English.** Notice the words that go together and how they are used in different situations. You can also write down the phrases that you find interesting or useful, and review them regularly.
- **Practice using phrases in your speech and writing.** You can try to use the phrases that you have learned in different contexts, such as

conversations, emails, essays, presentations, and so on. The more you use the phrases, the more comfortable and confident you will become with them.

The Journey to Mastering Spoken English

So, next time you're studying English, remember to pay attention to phrases, not just words. It might seem challenging at first, but with practice, you'll get the hang of it. And before you know it, you'll be speaking English more fluently and confidently.

Remember, mastering a language is a journey, not a destination. So, take your time, enjoy the process, and keep practising. You're doing great, and you'll get there! ☺

So, what do you think? Are you ready to start focusing on phrases? Trust me, it's a game-changer! Let's embark on this exciting journey together. You've got this!

👍 Phrases can help you to communicate more fluently, accurately, and confidently in your target language. They can also help you to understand spoken language better, as you can recognise familiar word combinations more easily than unfamiliar ones.

Key 5

Fillers

What Are Fillers?

In spoken English, fillers function as brief pauses or expressions utilised to help thinking, emphasise specific points or indicate shifts in a conversation's direction. These unobtrusive linguistic tools contribute significantly to fluid and efficient communication.

In the context of spoken English, fillers are often termed ***"hesitation devices" or "discourse markers"***. "They consist of words or phrases woven into conversations, presentations, or speeches, allowing speakers to briefly pause for thought, highlight essential information, or signal changes in the conversation's trajectory. Despite their seemingly minor role, a firm grasp of the appropriate use of fillers can notably enhance one's proficiency in spoken English.

Now, let's explore some common examples of filler words that you may encounter in everyday conversations:

1. **"Um" and "Uh":** These are perhaps the most ubiquitous filler words, used when someone is hesitating or searching for the right word. For example, "Um, I'm not sure if that's the case."

2. **"Like":** Often used in informal conversations, "like" can be a filler when it doesn't serve a clear grammatical function. "I was, like, so surprised."

3. **"You Know":** This phrase is used to check if the listener is following or to emphasise a point. "You know, I've been to that place before."

4. **"Well":** While "well" can be used appropriately, it's also a filler word when overused. "Well, I think we should, well, discuss this matter."

5. **"Basically":** Often used to simplify explanations, it can become a filler when used excessively. "Basically, what I'm trying to say is..."

6. **"Actually":** This word is used to emphasise a point or to clarify, but it can also slip into filler territory. "Actually, it's quite simple."

7. **"Literally":** Sometimes, people use "literally" as a filler word for added emphasis. "I was, like, literally blown away."

8. **"So"**: This word can be a filler when used to begin sentences without adding value. "So, I was thinking..."

9. **"Anyway"**: When used to transition between topics, "anyway" can turn into a filler. "So, anyway, what I wanted to say..."

10. **"Totally"**: Often used to express complete agreement or emphasis but can become a filler when overused. "I'm totally on board with that."

11. **"Well, you see"**: This phrase often serves as a filler when someone is about to explain something. "Well, you see, it all started..."

12. **"In a way"**: People use this phrase to add a level of vagueness or to hedge their statements. "In a way, I guess it makes sense."

13. **"To be honest"**: While it can be used to convey sincerity, it sometimes becomes a filler. "To be honest, I'm not sure."

14. **"As I was saying"**: Used as a transition, this phrase can occasionally slip into filler territory. "As I was saying, the point is..."

15. **"I mean"**: Often used to clarify or rephrase, it can also be a filler. "I mean, it's not that difficult."

16. **"On the other hand"**: Used in discussions to present an alternative perspective, it can be a filler

when overused. "On the other hand, you could also consider..."

17. **"It's like"**: This is used to make comparisons but can become a filler in casual conversation. "It's like, the best thing ever."

18. **"The thing is"**: Frequently used to emphasise a point, it can turn into a filler. "The thing is, you have to understand..."

19. **"So, umm..."**: A combination of "so" and "umm" is a common way to begin sentences with hesitation. "So, umm, what I wanted to say is..."

20. **"All in all"**: Often used to summarise, it can also serve as a filler. "All in all, it was a great experience."

One fundamental aspect that can increase your language proficiency is conquering filler words. These often underestimated linguistic hurdles, when effectively managed, can set you on the path to eloquent communication.

Let us explore key tips on managing filler words and how doing so can significantly elevate your English language skills.

Tip # 1: Recognise the Filler Words: The journey to conquering filler words starts with recognition. Common culprits include "um," "uh," "like," "you know," "well," "basically," "actually," and "literally." Identifying them in your speech is the first step to managing them.

Tip # 2: Replace Fillers with Pauses: Instead of habitually resorting to filler words during moments of thought, embrace the power of strategic pauses. These brief silences lend your speech a more deliberate and thoughtful quality.

Tip # 3: The Power of Practice and Awareness: Mastery often begins with repetition. Record your conversations or speeches to analyse your filler word usage. Self-awareness, combined with practice, allows you to gradually diminish their presence.

Tip # 4: Expand Your Glossary: Language proficiency is closely linked to vocabulary. Expanding your word bank enables you to express thoughts more precisely, reducing reliance on filler words. Embrace the richness of language to enhance your communication.

Tip # 5: Slow Down for Clarity: Fast speech often invites filler words. Slowing down your pace grants you the luxury of gathering thoughts and articulating them clearly. This directly impacts your overall language proficiency.

Tip # 6: Invest in Public Speaking Training: For those aiming at mastery in public speaking, enrolling in a public speaking course is invaluable. Such courses typically address filler word usage, providing techniques to overcome them.

Tip # 7: Seek Feedback and Reflect: Friends, colleagues, or mentors can provide invaluable feedback regarding your filler word usage. Self-reflection is equally essential in recognising and correcting this habit.

Tip # 8: The Art of Gestures: Replace filler words with gestures or body language to allow yourself a moment for thought when the temptation arises.

Tip # 9: Engage in Debates and Discussions: Practice is the crucible of language mastery. Engage in debates and discussions to train your mind in fluent expression without leaning on filler words.

Tip # 10: Embrace Active Listening: Proficient speakers often deploy filler words sparingly or not at all. Actively listening to their articulation can serve as a valuable learning experience.

Tip # 11: Analyse Your Speech: Transcribing and analysing a conversation or speech you've delivered can shed light on your filler word patterns. This exercise helps you identify areas for improvement.

Food for thought: In our talks, fillers are like our own speech fingerprints, giving each of us a unique sound. They're a bit like the brushstrokes on a canvas, adding a natural feel to our chats. But why do we use them so much? Are they just habits from our busy lives, helping us when we talk? Or do we throw them in on purpose, like adding flair to a painting? In those little "ums" and "uhs," we find the real heart of how we talk, making our mark in the big sea of conversation.

Key 6

Contractions

What Are Contractions?

In spoken English, contractions are shortened forms of two words combined into one. We use an apostrophe to show that some letters have been left out. For example, "I am" becomes "I'm," and "do not" becomes "don't."

Why Are Contractions Important in Spoken English?

Contractions are a big part of spoken English for a few important reasons:

1. **They Sound Natural**: Native English speakers always use contractions. When you use them too, it makes you sound more natural and like you know the language well.

2. **They Improve Flow:** Contractions help sentences flow smoothly. Long phrases can be a mouthful, and contractions make speaking easier and faster.

3. **They Show Informality:** Contractions are often used in informal conversations, showing you're relaxed and comfortable with the people you're talking to.

How to Use Contractions for English Learners:

For English learners, here's how to use contractions effectively:

- **Listen and Repeat:** Pay attention to how native speakers use contractions. Listen to music, watch movies, or have conversations to get used to them.

- **Practice Speaking**: Use contractions when you speak. Say "I'm" instead of "I am" or "they're" instead of "they are."

- **Know When to Use Them**: Contractions are more common in *casual, everyday speech*. Use them in conversations with **friends,** but use full words in formal situations like job *interviews or presentations.*

Remember, using contractions is a great way to make your spoken English sound natural and fluent. Practice makes perfect, so keep speaking and you'll get better at it!

Let's have a list of the most commonly used contractions in English:

1. I'm (I am)
2. you're (you are)
3. he's (he is)
4. she's (she is)
5. it's (it is)
6. we're (we are)
7. they're (they are)
8. can't (cannot)
9. don't (do not)
10. won't (will not)
11. isn't (is not)
12. hasn't (has not)
13. weren't (were not)

14. haven't (have not)
15. didn't (did not)
16. couldn't (could not)
17. shouldn't (should not)
18. wouldn't (would not)
19. doesn't (does not)
20. let's (let us)
21. that's (that is)
22. who's (who is)
23. what's (what is)
24. where's (where is)
25. when's (when is)
26. why's (why is)
27. how's (how is)
28. you've (you have)
29. they've (they have)
30. I've (I have)
31. she's (she has)
32. there's (there is)
33. here's (here is)
34. you'd (you would/you had)
35. he'd (he would/he had)
36. we'd (we would/we had)
37. she'd (she would/she had)
38. it'll (it will)
39. he'll (he will)
40. she'll (she will)
41. you'll (you will)
42. I'll (I will)
43. I'd (I would/I had)

44. there'll (there will)
45. we'll (we will)
46. haven't (have not)
47. didn't (did not)
48. aren't (are not)
49. should've (should have)
50. could've (could have)
51. would've (would have)
52. mightn't (might not)
53. mustn't (must not)
54. needn't (need not)
55. oughtn't (ought not)
56. shan't (shall not)
57. hasn't (has not)
58. doesn't (does not)
59. she's (she has)
60. we've (we have)
61. they've (they have)

Now let's see how Contractions can be formed in the English language in several cases:

1. **Subject + Verb Contraction:**

In this case, contractions are formed by combining a subject pronoun (I, you, he, she, it, we, they) with a verb.

- Examples: I'm (I am), you're (you are), he's (he is), she's (she is), we're (we are), they're (they are)

2. **Auxiliary Verb + Verb Contraction:**

Contractions can also occur with auxiliary verbs (helping verbs) like "will," "would," "could," "should," and "have." These contractions are often used when expressing future actions, conditional statements, or past actions.

  - Examples: can't (cannot), won't (will not), would've (would have), could've (could have)

3. **Negative Contractions:** Negations are formed by adding "not" to auxiliary verbs or main verbs. In spoken English, these combinations are often contracted for smoother and more natural speech.

  - Examples: can't (cannot), don't (do not), won't (will not), didn't (did not)

4. **Pronoun + Auxiliary Verb + Verb:**

Contractions can be formed when a subject pronoun is combined with an auxiliary verb (usually "have") and a main verb. These contractions are common in questions and negative statements.

  - Examples: I've (I have), you've (you have), they've (they have)

5. **Verb + Pronoun Contraction**: In some cases, a verb is combined with a pronoun (usually "is" or "has") to create a contraction.

  - Examples: she's (she has), he's (he is)

6. **Compound Forms:** Contractions can be used in compound words like "let's" (let us) and "that's" (that is).

   - Examples: let's (let us), that's (that is)

7. **Informal Speech**: Contractions are frequently used in informal spoken English. When people chat, tell stories, or engage in everyday conversation, they naturally use contractions to make their speech more relaxed and fluid.

These are typical cases in which contractions are used in English. While they are prevalent in spoken language, it's essential to recognise when and how to use them appropriately, as they are less common in formal writing or professional contexts.

Practice Sheet: Use contractions wherever necessary:

1. I **have not** seen him in ages; he **has** been travelling for work.
2. She **is** going to join us for dinner later; we **are** meeting at the new restaurant downtown.
3. I **do not** think they **will** be able to make it to the party; they **have** got a prior commitment.
4. I **cannot** believe it **is** already Friday; the week has flown by.
5. They **will not** be here on time; there **is** heavy traffic on the main road.
6. I'm looking forward to the weekend; I **have** planned a relaxing day at home.

Key 7

Reductions in English

While talking about spoken English and getting fluent, one interesting thing that can help you improve your language skills is the use of reductions. When people talk, they often change words and phrases into more casual, often colloquial versions. These are called reductions. These shortcuts can make your spoken English sound more natural and casual while also helping you understand native speakers better. We will learn how to recognise and use reductions, like "gonna" for "going" and "wanna" for "want to," as powerful tools to improve your spoken language.) Understanding these reductions can indeed be a key to unlocking the nuances of spoken English. Let's start:

Imagine you are listening to a fast-paced (speedy) conversation between two English speakers. You might hear words like 'gonna', 'wanna', and 'kinda' being used frequently. These words might sound unfamiliar, but they're actually just **shortened versions** of longer phrases used to make speech quicker and more fluid.

- When someone says **'gonna'**, they mean "going to". So, if you hear "I'm gonna go", it's the same as "I'm going to go".

- The word **'wanna'** is short for "want to". So, "I wanna know!" is a casual way of saying "I want to know!".

Lastly, **'kinda'** is a contraction of "kind of", used to indicate something is somewhat or to some degree. For example, "I'm kinda tired" means "I'm somewhat tired".

These shortened phrases, known as **reductions**, are a common feature of spoken English, especially in informal, casual conversations. However, they're typically avoided in formal writing or professional settings.

So, the next time you listen to a conversation in English, keep an ear out for these reductions. Understanding them will help you follow along and even participate more naturally in the conversation. Happy learning!

Let us have more of **Reductions**:

1. **I've gottagotəthə**: This is a reduction of I have got to go to the store after work.

2. **Mosta:** This is a reduced form of the words most and of. For example, Mosta the engagement with our brand comes from Instagram.

3. **Lotta**: This is a reduced form of a lot of. For example, I have a lotta work to do.

4. **Tellem:** This is a reduction of tell him. For example, Can you tellem to call me?

5. **Didja**: This is a reduction of did you. For example, Didja finish the report?

6. **Wantsta**: This is a reduction of wants to. For example, He wantsta stay home.

7. **Reada, Hasa, Mada**: These are reductions of read a, has a, made a respectively. For example, I reada good book, She has a car, Wemada mess.

Remember, these reductions are a characteristic feature of spoken English and are often used in casual, fast-paced speech. However, they are considered informal and are typically not used in formal writing or professional settings.

Let's have more of it:

1. **Gimme** (Give me).
2. **Kinda** (Kind of)
3. *Sorta** (Sort of)
4. *Lemme** (Let me)
5. **Dunno** (Don't know)
6. **Ain't** (Am not / Is not / Are not)
7. **Hafta** (Have to)
8. . **Shoulda** (Should have)
9. **Coulda** (Could have)
10. **Woulda** (Would have)
11. . **Musta** (Must have)
12. . **Oughta** (Ought to)
13. . **Mighta** (Might have)

14. . **Outta** (Out of)
15. . **Y'all** (You all)
16. . **Howdy** (How do you do)
17. . **Fella** (Fellow)
18. . **Cuz** (Because)
19. . **Y'know** (You know)
20. . **Whatcha** (What are you)
21. . **Where'd** (Where did)
22. . **What's up** (What is up)
23. **I'mma** (I'm going to)
24. *Yummy** (Delicious)
25 **Fave** (Favorite)
26. **C'mon** (Come on)
27.. **Betcha** (Bet you)

Read the following conversation and see where Reduction can be used

Amy: Hey, what are you up to this weekend?

Tom: Not much, just going to chill at home. You?

Amy: Same here. Do you **want to** catch a movie or something?

Tom: Sounds good! I **have to** finish some work in the morning, but I am free in the afternoon.

Amy: No worries. Let us meet up around 3 at the cinema.

Tom: Cool, I will see you then. Anything specific you **want to** watch?

Key 8

Proverbs and Common Sayings in English

How They Help You Speak Better

Proverbs and common sayings are like gems in the treasure box of language. They are short, wise, and memorable expressions that convey essential truths and cultural wisdom. In the context of spoken English, understanding and using proverbs and common sayings can greatly enhance your language skills and communication. Here's why they are so useful:

1. **Say More with Less**: Proverbs and sayings are like shortcuts. They help you say complicated things in a simple way. For example, saying, "Don't count your chickens before they hatch", means don't make big plans before you're sure they will happen.

2. **Learn about Culture:** These phrases often come from the history and beliefs of a culture. Learning them can help you understand the people and their way of thinking. It's like a key to their world.

3. **Fit In** When you use proverbs and sayings, it makes you sound like you belong. People like to talk to someone who speaks like they do.

4. Make Conversations More Interesting: These phrases add spice to your talk. People enjoy listening when you use them. For example, saying "Every cloud has a silver lining" can make someone feel better when things aren't going well.

5. Show Your Feelings: You can use these sayings to express your feelings. Whether you're happy or sad, there's a saying for it. For example, "The ball is in your court" means someone has control.

6. Be Seen as Smart: Using proverbs and sayings can make you look clever. People will think you know a lot about English. This can help in school or work.

7. Remember and Learn: Learning these phrases is good for your memory and vocabulary. You will remember not only the saying but also when to use it. It's like growing your language skills.

So, don't *ignore proverbs and sayings*. They are your secret tools for better spoken English. They make you sound interesting, help you connect with others, and show that you know your stuff. Start learning them, and your English will shine

Let us have some famous proverbs commonly used or spoken/ heard in our conversations.

1. **A Bird in the Hand Is Worth Two in the Bush:**

    - Advocating for the appreciation of present, assured advantages over uncertain future prospects.

2. **A Penny for Your Thoughts:**

   - A whimsical inquiry seeking insight into one's current musings or contemplations.

3. **A Picture Is Worth a Thousand Words:**

   - Acknowledging the expressive power of visual representation surpassing verbal or written descriptions.

4. **A Stitch in Time Saves Nine:**

   - Urging timely resolution to prevent a minor issue from escalating into a major problem.

5. **A watched pot never boils:**

   - Conveying the perception that time feels prolonged when one is eagerly awaiting an outcome.

6. **Absence Makes the Heart Grow Fonder:**

   - Suggesting increased affection or appreciation in the absence of someone or something.

7. **Actions Speak Louder Than Words:**

   - People's true intentions manifest through deeds rather than mere words.

8. **All is fair in love and war:**

- Expressing the idea that certain actions, even morally questionable ones, are justifiable in extreme situations.

9. **All That Ends Well is Well:**

- Affirming that a positive conclusion justifies the preceding events or efforts.

10. **All That Glitters Is Not Gold:**

- Cautioning against the assumption that all things attractive or impressive are inherently valuable or genuine.

11. **Beauty is in the eye of the beholder:**

- Acknowledging the subjectivity of aesthetic judgments, varying from person to person.

12. **Better Late Than Never:**

- Timeliness may elude, but tardy actions still hold value compared to inaction.

13. **Better Safe Than Sorry:**

- Encouraging a cautious approach to avoid potential regrets or adverse consequences.

14. **Barking Up the Wrong Tree:**

- Engaging in a fruitless pursuit, directing focus amiss, or mistakenly attributing blame.

15. **Beat Around the Bush:**

- Circumventing the crux of the matter, avoiding direct discourse on the issue at hand.

16. **Beauty is Only Skin Deep:**

    - Emphasizing the idea that true beauty goes beyond external appearances, highlighting the importance of inner qualities.

17. **Beggars Can't Be Choosers:**

    - Implying a lack of entitlement when seeking assistance or favours from others.

18. **Better Safe Than Sorry:**

    - Advocating a prudent and cautious approach to avoid potential regrets or unforeseen consequences.

19. **Birds of a Feather Flock Together:**

    - Affirming the tendency for like-minded individuals to associate or form groups.

20. **Break a Leg:**

- An unconventional wish for good fortune or success in a forthcoming endeavour.

21. **Call It a Day:**

    - Cease endeavours for the present, acknowledging a task's completion or the need for a hiatus.

22. **Cleanliness is Next to Godliness:**

- Advocating the virtue of cleanliness and orderliness is often associated with moral purity.

23. **Cut Corners:**

- Sacrificing quality for expedience, opting for shortcuts to save time or resources.

24. **Don't Bite the Hand That Feeds You:**

- Advising against harming those who provide support or assistance.

25. **Don't Count Your Chickens Before They Hatch:**

- Cautioning against making plans based on uncertain events that may or may not come to fruition.

26. **Don't Cry Over Spilled Milk:**

- Advising against dwelling on past mistakes or unfortunate events that cannot be undone.

27. **Don't Judge a Book by Its Cover:**

- Cautioning against forming opinions based solely on outward appearances.

28. **Don't Put All Your Eggs in One Basket:**

- Diversify efforts and resources, avoiding concentration in a singular venture to avert potential loss.

29. Don't Put the Cart Before the Horse:

- Encouraging a methodical approach, ensuring tasks are performed in the correct sequence.

30. Don't Put the Toothpaste Back in the Tube:

- Emphasizing the irreversible nature of certain actions once taken.

31. Don't Cry Over Spilled Milk:

- Don't waste time on things you can't change.

32. Every Cloud Has a Silver Lining:

- Optimism in adversity, anticipating positive outcomes from challenging situations.

33. Every Dog Has Its Day:

- Asserting that everyone will experience a period of good fortune or success.

34. Every Man for Himself:

- Suggesting a self-reliant attitude where individuals prioritize their own interests in challenging situations.

35. Fortune Favors the Bold/brave:

- Celebrating the courage of those who pursue their goals with audacity and determination.

36. **Get Out of Hand:**

- Losing control, witnessing a situation escalate beyond manageable bounds.

37. **Give Someone the Cold Shoulder:**

- Purposefully ignoring or snubbing an individual.

38. **Go Back to the Drawing Board:**

- Commencing anew, often after recognizing flaws or inadequacies in a prior approach.

39. **Good Things Come to Those Who Wait:**

- Advocating patience, asserting that waiting can lead to rewarding outcomes.

40. **Haste Makes Waste:**

- Rushing leads to mistakes.

41. **Home is Where the Heart Is:**

- Expressing the comfort and familiarity of one's own abode.

42. **If It Ain't Broke, Don't Fix It:**

- Discouraging unnecessary alterations to something functioning adequately.

43. **If the Cap Fits, Wear It:**

- Encouraging individuals to accept criticism or acknowledge a truth if it applies to them.

44. If You Play With Fire, You'll Get Burned:

- Warning against engaging in risky endeavours that may result in adverse consequences.

45. In the Heat of the Moment:

- Acting impulsively or emotionally, influenced by immediate circumstances.

46. It's a Drop in the Bucket:

- Describing a contribution or action that is relatively small compared to the overall context.

47. It's Not Rocket Science:

- Asserting that a task or concept is not overly complex and can be easily grasped.

48. It's Raining Cats and Dogs:

- Describing heavy rainfall or an intense downpour.

49. Keep Your Friends Close and Your Enemies Closer:

- Encouraging strategic vigilance by staying close to potential adversaries to monitor their actions.

50. Kill Two Birds With One Stone:

- Achieving dual objectives with a singular effort.

51. Let Sleeping Dogs Lie:

- Avoid stirring up old problems.

52. Like Father, Like Son:

- Noting the tendency for children to exhibit characteristics or behaviours similar to their parents.

53. Look Before You Leap:

- Encouraging careful consideration and planning before taking significant actions.

54. Many Hands Make Light Work:

- Tasks are easier when many people help.

55. Misery Loves Company:

- Noting the tendency for unhappy individuals to find solace in the shared unhappiness of others.

56. Money Doesn't Grow on Trees:

- Reminding that financial resources are not limitless and should be managed judiciously.

57. No Man is an Island:

- Emphasizing the universal need for companionship and social connections.

58. **No Pain, No Gain:**

- Emphasizing the necessity of exertion and hardship for eventual success.

59. **Once in a Blue Moon:**

- Infrequent occurrences, rare events transpiring at irregular intervals.

60. **One Man's Trash is Another Man's Treasure:**

- What's useless to one person may be valuable to another.

61. **Out of Sight, Out of Mind:**

- Suggesting that things or people not in immediate awareness are easily forgotten or ignored.

62. **People Who Live in Glass Houses Should Not Throw Stones:**

- Discouraging criticism when one possesses similar vulnerabilities.

63. **Piece of Cake:**

- Tasks or endeavours characterised by simplicity and ease.

64. **Practice Makes Perfect:**

- Repeating an activity makes you better at it.

65. **Rome Wasn't Built in a Day:**

- Acknowledging the time and effort required for significant achievements.

66. **See Eye to Eye:**

- Mutual agreement or shared perspective between individuals.

67. **Silence is Golden:**

- Sometimes it's best to say nothing.

68. **Sit on the Fence:**

- Hesitating to make a decision or take a stance, remaining neutral.

69. **Speak of the Devil!:**

- Uttered when a person, recently discussed, unexpectedly appears.

70. **Take It With a Grain of Salt:**

- Treating information or advice with scepticism, not wholly relying on its accuracy.

71. **The Best of Both Worlds:**

- An ideal scenario where one can enjoy the benefits of two different opportunities simultaneously.

72. The Devil is in the Details:

- Highlighting the importance of paying attention to small, often overlooked, details that can lead to problems.

73. The Grass is Always Greener on the Other Side:

- Expressing the common tendency to desire what others possess, overlooking potential drawbacks.

74. The Pen is Mightier Than the Sword:

- Highlighting the persuasive power of words and ideas over forceful actions.

75. The Pot Calling the Kettle Black:

- Describing a situation where someone accuses another of a fault they themselves possess.

76. The Proof is in the Pudding:

- Asserting that the real value or success of something becomes evident when put to practical tests.

77. There's No Place Like Home:

- Expressing the comfort and familiarity of one's own abode.

78. **There's No Smoke Without Fire:**

- Suggesting that rumours or suspicions often have some basis in truth.

79. **Time Flies When You're Having Fun:**

- Time seems to pass quickly when you're enjoying yourself.

80. **Too Many Cooks Spoil the Broth:**

- Advising against an excess of opinions or individuals involved in a decision-making process.

81. **Two Heads Are Better Than One:**

- Advocating collaboration, suggesting that joint efforts are more effective than individual endeavours.

82. **Two Wrongs Don't Make a Right:**

- Emphasizing that retaliatory actions do not solve problems or justify wrongdoing.

83. **Under the Weather:**

- Feeling unwell or indisposed, experiencing a state of mild illness.

84. **When in Rome, Do as the Romans Do:**

- Encouraging adherence to local customs and norms when in a foreign environment.

85. Where There's Smoke, There's Fire:

- Indicating that suspicion or rumours may be indicative of an underlying problem.

86. You Can Lead a Horse to Water, But You Can't Make Him Drink:

- Recognizing the limitations of providing opportunities if individuals are unwilling to seize them.

87. You Can't Judge a Book by Its Cover:

- Cautioning against forming opinions based solely on outward appearances.

88. You Can't Make an Omelet Without Breaking Eggs:

- Acknowledging that significant achievements may involve overcoming obstacles or making sacrifices.

89. You Can't Make a Silk Purse Out of a Sow's Ear:

- Stating that one cannot turn something of low quality into something high quality.

90. You Can't Put the Toothpaste Back in the Tube:

- Emphasizing the irreversible nature of certain actions once taken.

91. **You Can't Run With the Hare and Hunt With the Hounds:**

   - Advising against attempting to support conflicting parties or positions.

92. **You Can't Squeeze Blood From a Stone:**
   - Signifying the impossibility of extracting something from a source that lacks it.

93. **You Can't Make Bricks Without Straw:**
   - Emphasizing the necessity of having the required materials to accomplish a task.

94. **You Catch More Flies With Honey Than With Vinegar:**

Key 9

Collocations

Mastering Spoken English: The Power of Collocations
Hello, aspiring English speakers! Today, we're going to explore an interesting aspect of the English language that can significantly develop your fluency - **collocations**.

What are Collocations?

In simple terms, collocations are **words that often go together/frequently appear together.** They're like best friends in the language world, rarely seen apart. For example, we say 'fast food', not 'quick food'. Similarly, we 'take a shower', not 'do a shower'. We say 'brush your teeth' instead of 'clean your teeth' or 'make a mistake' rather than 'do a mistake'. These word pairs sound 'right' to native English speakers because they're used to hearing them together.

Why are Collocations Important?

Knowing collocations can make your English sound more natural and fluent. It's not just about knowing vocabulary, but also understanding how words connect and interact. This is especially crucial in spoken English, where fluency and flow are essential.

Collocations: The Key to Fluency

By understanding and using collocations, you can make your spoken English sound more fluent and natural. It's like having a secret weapon in your language arsenal!

So, dear students/Learners, start paying attention to collocations. Listen for them in conversations, look for them in books, and practice using them in your speech. Remember, mastering collocations is a sure-fire way to develop your spoken English skills.

Let's see some examples of collocations across different categories:

1. **Adjective + Noun Collocations:**
   o Bright sunshine
   o Severe consequences
   o Major problem
   o Strong coffee
   o Heavy rain
   o Deep thought
   o High temperature
   o Fast car
   o Old friend
   o Large crowd
2. **Verb + Noun Collocations:**
   o **Catch a cold**
   o Pay attention
   o Save time
   o Take a shower
   o Make a decision
   o Do homework
   o Break a record

- - Keep a promise
  - Hold a meeting
  - Lose weight
  -

3. Noun + Noun Collocations:

- - Heart and soul
  - Law and order
  - Trial and error
  - Bread and butter
  - Fish and chips
  - Peace and quiet
  - Salt and pepper
  - Cause and effect
  - Supply and demand
  - Crime and punishment
  -

4. Adverb + Adjective Collocations:

- - Rapidly increasing
  - Completely wrong
  - Partially correct
  - Highly successful
  - Deeply regrettable
  - Fully aware
  - Extremely happy
  - Totally unexpected
  - Absolutely perfect
  - Entirely possible
  -

5. Verb + Adverb Collocations:

- - Drive slowly
  - Think quickly

- o   Eat slowly
- o   Speak softly
- o   Work hard
- o   Laugh loudly
- o   Run fast
- o   Listen carefully
- o   Arrive early
- o   Talk loudly

These are just a few examples. The English language has a vast number of collocations, and learning them can significantly improve your fluency and comprehension. ☺

Now let's get deeper into it. I strongly believe that familiarising oneself with the following collocations will not only increase your / solve your problem of ' word Shortage' but also help you express yourself better.

Everyday Life:

1. Catch the bus/train

2. Grab a bite

3. Run errands

4. Make a phone call

5. Take a shower

6. Have a nap

7. Pay attention

8. Keep a promise

9. Break the news

10. Lose touch

11.

Work and Career:

11. Land a job

12. Meet a deadline

13. Take a break

14. Forge a career

15. Hone your skills

16. Strike a deal

17. Hold a meeting

18. Make a decision

19. Give a presentation

20. Get a promotion

Education:

21. Pursue studies

22. Pass an exam

23. Take notes

24. Face challenges

25. Miss a class

26. Submit an assignment

27. Acquire knowledge

28. Excel in a subject

29. Fulfil requirements

30. Attend a lecture

Social Interactions:

31. Hang out with friends

32. Strike up a conversation

33. Make an impression

34. Keep in touch

35. Build relationships

36. Share a laugh

37. Give compliments

38. Offer assistance

39. Attend a party

40. Maintain friendship

Emotions and Feelings:

41. Bear in mind
42. Express gratitude
43. Feel under the weather
44. Face disappointment
45. Show appreciation
46. Voice concerns

47.   Harbour doubts
48.   Handle stress
49.   Take up a hobby
51.   Develop a skill
52.   Set goals
53.   Overcome obstacles
54.   Foster creativity
55.   Embrace change
56.   Seize opportunities
57.   Embark on a journey
58.   Learn from experiences
59.   Cultivate resilience

Technology and Communication:

61.   Send an email
62.   Receive a message
63.   Make a video call
64.   Update social media
65.   Browse the internet
66.   Download an app
67.   Upload a file
68.   Install software
69.   Navigate a website
70.   Create a profile

Travel and Exploration:

71.   Embark on a journey
72.   Book accommodation

73. Explore new places
74. Take a trip
75. Go sightseeing
76. Experience culture
77. Capture memories
78. Plan an itinerary

Health and Well-being:

81. Maintain a healthy lifestyle
82. Follow a diet
83. Undergo a check-up
84. Suffer from allergies
85. Overcome illness
86. Practice mindfulness
87. Stay physically active
88. Boost mental well-being
89. Seek medical advice
90. Adopt healthy habits

Environment and Sustainability:

91. Reduce carbon footprint
92. Conserve natural resources
93. Recycle waste
94. Promote sustainability
95. Combat climate change
96. Protect biodiversity
97. Support eco-friendly initiatives
98. Raise environmental awareness

99. Implement green practices

100. Live a sustainable lifestyle

Culinary Delights:

101. Cook a meal

102. Taste a delicacy

103. Savour the flavour

104. Try a new recipe

105. Prepare a feast

106. Share a meal

107. Indulge in desserts

108. Brew a cup of tea

109. Sip a refreshing drink

110. Crave a snack

Relationships and Family:

111. Build a family

112. Raise children

113. Create lasting memories

114. Celebrate milestones

115. Offer emotional support

116. Resolve conflicts

117. Cherish moments

118. Express affection

119. Nurture relationships

120. Celebrate achievements

Finance and Money:

121.   Save money
122.   Invest wisely
123.

Budget carefully

124.   Earn a salary
125.   Pay bills
126.   Secure a loan
127.   Handle finances
128.   Make a purchase
129.   Manage expenses
130.   Plan for retirement

Fashion and Style:

131.   Choose an outfit
132.   Wear accessories

133.   Follow fashion trends
134.   Express personal style
135.   Shop for clothing
136.   Mix and match
137.   Coordinate colours

138.   Accessorize appropriately
139.   Create a signature look

Arts and Creativity:

141.   Create art
142.   Attend a performance
143.   Appreciate aesthetics

144.   Compose music
145.   Write poetry
146.   Capture moments in photography
147.   Dance to the rhythm
148.   Act in a play
149.   Sculpt with clay
150.   Express artistic vision

Legal and Governance:

151.   Obey the law
152.   Exercise legal rights
153.   Seek legal advice
154.   Sign a contract
155.   Negotiate terms
156.   Settle dispute
157.   Serve on a jury
158.   Commit a crime
159.   Face legal consequences
160.   Enforce regulations

Hobbies and Leisure:

161.   Play a musical instrument
162.   Engage in outdoor activities
163.   Read a book
164.   Watch a movie
165.   Attend a concert
166.   Explore nature
167.   Join a club
168.   Play sports
169.   Solve puzzles
170.   Participate in events

171. Use advanced technology
172. Analyse data
173. Apply scientific principles
174. Explore technological advancements

Weather and Seasons:

181. Experience sunshine
182. Face a storm
183. Enjoy a breeze
184. Endure extreme heat
185. Welcome rainfall
186. Witness a snowfall
187. Embrace winter warmth
188. Forecast the weather
189. Chase a rainbow
190. Admire a sunset

Sports and Fitness:

191. Play a sport
192. Train regularly
193. Score a goal
194. Attend a match
195. Compete in a tournament
196. Follow a fitness routine
197. Achieve personal best
198. Support a team
199. Cheer for athletes
200. Lead a healthy lifestyle

Transportation:

201.   Commute to work
202.   Drive a vehicle
203.   Navigate traffic
204.   Board a flight
205.   Ride a bicycle
206.   Take public transport
207.   Book a ticket
208.   Embark on a journey
209.   Hitch a ride
210.   Arrange transportation
211.

Achievements and Success:

211.   Attain a goal
212.   Excel in a field
213.   Celebrate success
214.   Reach milestones
215.   Fulfil dreams
216.   Overcome challenges
217.   Secure achievements
218.   Realize potential
219.   Master a skill
220.   Strive for excellence

Challenges and Obstacles:

221.   Face adversity
222.   Overcome hurdles
223.   Tackle challenges
224.   Navigate obstacles
225.   Confront difficulties
226.   Handle setbacks
227.   Endure hardships

228. Conquer fears
229. Learn from failures
230. Adapt to changes

Holidays and Festivals:

231. Celebrate a festival
232. Exchange gifts
233. Decorate the house
234. Host a gathering
235. Cook festive meals
236. Attend holiday events
237. Create traditions
238. Send greetings
239. Experience holiday cheer
240. Share festive joy

Food and Dining:

241. Cook a recipe
242. Dine in a restaurant
243. Savour flavours
244. Try local cuisine
245. Prepare a feast
246. Enjoy a meal
247. Share a dish
248. Taste a delicacy
249. Explore culinary delights
250. Order takeout
251.

Music and Entertainment:

251. Play an instrument
252. Compose music

253. Attend a concert
254. Listen to a playlist
255. Dance to the rhythm
256. Watch a performance
257. Sing along
258. Appreciate live music
259. Explore new genres
260. Create a music collection
261.

Relationships and Romance:

261. Build a connection
262. Share intimate moments
263. Express love
264. Plan romantic gestures
265. Commit to a relationship
266. Navigate relationship dynamics
267. Celebrate anniversaries
268. Overcome relationship challenges
269. Appreciate a partner
270. Create lasting memories

Nature and Outdoors:

271. Explore nature
272. Hike in the mountains
273. Camp under the stars
274. Enjoy a scenic view
275. Walk in the woods
276. Observe wildlife

277.	Stroll on the beach
278.	Plant a garden
279.	Picnic in the park
280.	Capture the sunrise

Personality Traits:

281.	Display confidence
282.	Exhibit resilience
283.	Radiate positivity
284.	Demonstrate empathy
285.	Embrace uniqueness
286.	Cultivate humility
287.	Express creativity
288.	Embody authenticity
289.	Radiate charm
290.	Project sincerity

Mind and Thought:

291.	Have second thoughts
292.	Ponder a decision
293.	Reflect on experiences
294.	Consider possibilities
295.	Contemplate the future
296.	Weigh the pros and cons
297.	Engage in critical thinking
298.	Formulate ideas
299.	Process information
300.	Challenge assumptions

Cultural and Social Issues:

| 301. | Address social issues |
| 302. | Promote inclusivity |

303. Advocate for equality
304. Raise awareness
305. Support a cause
306. Engage in community service
307. Contribute to social change
308. Challenge stereotypes
309. Celebrate diversity
310. Foster cultural understanding

Fashion and Appearance:

311. Choose an outfit
312. Accessorize a look
313. Style hair
314. Experiment with fashion
315. Coordinate colours
316. Follow fashion trends
317. Wear makeup
318. Shop for clothing
319. Create a signature look
320. Express personal style

Time and Scheduling:

321. Plan an itinerary
322. Meet deadlines
323. Schedule appointments
324. Manage time effectively
325. Prioritize tasks
326. Allocate time wisely
327. Set a timeline
328. Stick to a schedule
329. Reschedule plans
330. Block out time

Books and Literature:

331.	Read a novel
332.	Write a book
333.	Explore literary genres
334.	Discuss a plot
335.	Attend a book club
336.	Borrow a library book
337.	Publish a work
338.	Analyse characters
339.	Appreciate symbolism
340.	Quote literature

Art and Creativity:

341.	Create art
342.	Attend an exhibition
343.	Appreciate aesthetics
344.	Sketch a drawing
345.	Compose music
346.	Capture moments in photography
347.	Write poetry
348.	Sculpt with clay
349.	Express artistic vision
350.	Explore creativity

Health and Fitness:

351.	Maintain a healthy lifestyle
352.	Follow a fitness routine
353.	Adopt healthy habits
354.	Practice mindfulness
355.	Set health goals
356.	Achieve fitness milestones

357. Balance physical and mental well-being
358. Embrace a holistic approach
359. Nurture overall health
360. Pursue well-being

Challenges and Growth:

361. Face personal challenges
362. Embrace growth
363. Learn from setbacks
364. Overcome obstacles
365. Adapt to change
366. Develop resilience
367. Cultivate perseverance
368. Celebrate progress
369. Pursue personal development
370. Explore new horizons

Dreams and Aspirations:

371. Chase dreams
372. Set ambitious goals
373. Pursue passions
374. Fulfill aspirations
375. Realize potential
376. Live out fantasies
377. Visualise success
378. Turn dreams into reality
379. Aim for the stars
380. Strive for greatness

381.

Learning and Education:

381.	Pursue knowledge
382.	Attend lectures
383.	Engage in discussions
384.	Explore educational opportunities
385.	Seek intellectual growth
386.	Participate in workshops
387.	Complete assignments
388.	Excel academically
389.	Collaborate on projects

Key 10

Words Going in Pairs (Binomials)

Have you ever wondered why we say "black and white" instead of "white and black", or why we say "bread and butter" and not "butter and bread"? It's not just a random choice, but a fascinating aspect of the English language known as **binomial** pairs or "Words Going in Pairs".

Binomial pairs are pairs of words that are joined by a conjunction, usually "and" or "or". The order of these words is fixed, it's always "salt and pepper", never "pepper and salt". This is one of the keys to sounding natural in English.

For example, we say "ladies and gentlemen", not "gentlemen and ladies". We say **"trick or treat"**, not "treat or trick". We say "rock and roll", not "roll and rock".

Why is this order so important? Well, it's all about rhythm, melody, and how the language flows. English, like music, has its own rhythm and melody. When the words in a pair flow well together, they're pleasing to the ear.

So, next time you're learning English, pay attention to these binomial pairs. They'll not only help you sound more natural, but they'll also give you a deeper understanding of the rhythm and melody of English. Remember, it's not just about the words you use, but also how you use them. So, let's rock and roll with English!

Let's have a list of **binomial pairs:**

1. **Black and white:** The rules are as clear as **black and white**.

2. **Bread and butter:** Writing is my **bread and butter**.

3. **Salt and pepper:** They go together like **salt and pepper**.

4. **Fish and chips:** When in England, you must try **fish and chips**.

5. **Trial and error:** We found the solution through **trial and error**.

6. **Supply and demand:** The price of goods depends on **supply and demand**.

7. **Pros and cons:** Let's weigh the **pros and cons** before making a decision.

8. **Sick and tired:** I'm **sick and tired** of all this noise.

9. **Now or never:** It's **now or never**, we must act quickly.

10. **Dead or alive:** They promised a reward for the return of the lost dog, **dead or alive**.

11. **Wait and see:** We'll just have to **wait and see** what happens.

12. **Lost and Found:** I **found** your keys in the **lost and found**.

13. **Sweet and sour:** Life is full of **sweet and sour** moments.

14. **Heart and soul:** I put my **heart and soul** into this project.

15. **Question and answer:** After the presentation, there will be a **question and answer** session.

16. **Ladies and gentlemen: Ladies and gentlemen**, please take your seats.

17. **First and foremost: First and foremost**, safety is our priority.

18. **Pen and paper:** Sometimes, all you need is a **pen and paper** to jot down your thoughts.

19. **Soap and water:** All you need to clean your hands is **soap and water**.

20. **Knife and fork:** In Western cultures, people often use a **knife and fork** to eat.

21. **Thunder and lightning:** The **thunder and lightning** scared the children.

22. **Song and dance:** He made a big **song and dance** about his promotion.

23. **Rest and relaxation:** Everyone needs some **rest and relaxation** from time to time.

24. **Husband and wife:** They have been **husband and wife** for 50 years.

25. **Sunrise and sunset:** The **sunrise and sunset** are beautiful on the beach.

26. **Young and old:** The game is enjoyed by **young and old** alike.

27. **Hot and cold:** The weather here can be **hot and cold**.

28. **Here and there:** I've been **travelling here and there** for work.

29. **Up and down:** He's been feeling **up and down** lately.

30. **Give and take:** A good relationship involves a lot of **give and take**.

31. **Law and order:** We need **law and order** to maintain a peaceful society.

32. **Peace and quiet:** I moved to the countryside for some **peace and quiet**.

33. **Rise and shine: Rise and shine**, it's a beautiful morning!

34. **Short and sweet:** Keep your speech **short and sweet**.

35. **Tried and tested:** This is a **tried and tested** method for success.

36. **Wine and dine:** He promised to **wine and dine** me.

37. **Bits and pieces:** I've been collecting **bits and pieces** for my scrapbook.

38. **Down and out:** He was **down and out** after losing his job. **High and dry:** The sudden departure of their mother left them **high and dry**.

39. **Leaps and bounds:** My garden has grown in **leaps and bounds** this year.

40. **Neat and tidy:** Keep your room **neat and tidy**.

41. **Part and parcel:** Being recognised on the street is **part and parcel** of being a celebrity.

42. **Rough and ready:** The accommodations were **rough and ready**.

43. **Spick and span:** I like to keep my kitchen **spick and span**.

44. **Through thick and thin:** My best friend has been with me **through thick and thin**.

45. **To and fro:** The pendulum swings **to and fro**.

46. **Wear and tear:** The car has suffered a lot of **wear and tear** over the years.

47. **Cut and dried:** The rules are **cut and dried**.

48. **Down and dirty:** They got **down and dirty** in the mud.

49. **Hale and hearty:** My grandfather is **hale and hearty** at the age of 90.

50. **Kith and kin:** I invited all my **kith and kin** to the wedding.

51. **Nook and cranny:** I searched every **nook and cranny** but couldn't find my keys.

52. **Pride and joy:** My children are my **pride and joy**.

53. **Rant and rave:** He would **rant and rave** about the smallest things.

54. **Safe and sound:** The lost hikers were found **safe and sound**.

55. **Tops and tails:** We need to wear **tops and tails** to the wedding.

56. **Ups and downs:** Every relationship has its **ups and downs**.

57. **Wild and woolly:** The party got a bit **wild and woolly**.

58. **Willy-nilly:** Decisions cannot be made **willy-nilly**.

59. **Zig and zag:** The rabbit would **zig and zag** to avoid the fox.

60. **Null and void:** The contract was declared **null and void**.

61. **Pick and choose:** You can't always **pick and choose** your assignments.

62. **Rack and ruin:** The house has gone to **rack and ruin** since no one lives there.

63. **Sink or swim:** It's **sink or swim** time - either we succeed in this venture or we fail.

64. **Toss and turn:** I was **tossing and turning** all night, worrying about the exam.

65. **Wax and wane:** The moon **waxes and wanes** every month.

66. **Bells and whistles:** The new model of the car has all the **bells and whistles**.

67. **Fair and square:** I won the game **fair and square**.

68. **Hustle and bustle:** I love the **hustle and bustle** of the city.

69. **Odds and ends:** I've been sorting through the **odds and ends** in the garage.

70. **Pots and pans:** I cleaned all the **pots and pans** after dinner.

71. **Aches and pains:** As I get older, I'm starting to feel various **aches and pains**.

72. **Bright and early:** I have to wake up **bright and early** for work tomorrow.

73. **Dead and buried:** That old disagreement is **dead and buried**; let's not bring it up again.

74. **Ebb and flow:** The **ebb and flow** of the tides is a natural phenomenon.

75. **Fast and Furious:** The questions came **fast and furious** during the quiz.

76. **Grin and bear it:** I don't like my job, but I have to **grin and bear it**.

77. **Hale and hearty:** My grandparents are still **hale and hearty** in their eighties.

78. **Ins and outs:** She knows the **ins and outs** of this business.

79. **Jack of all trades:** He's a **jack of all trades**, skilled at many things.

80. **Kith and kin:** I invited all my **kith and kin** to the wedding.

81. **Live and learn:** I made a mistake, but I'll **live and learn**.

82. **Make or mar:** This decision could **make or mar** our chances of success.

83. **Nuts and bolts:** Let's get down to the **nuts and bolts** of the plan.

84. **Out and about** It's a beautiful day to be **out and about**.

85. **Prim and proper:** She's always so **prim and proper**, never a hair out of place.

86. **Quick and easy:** This recipe is **quick and easy** to make.

87. **Rough and ready:** The prototype is **rough and ready** but it works.

88. **Safe and secure:** The documents are **safe and secure** in the vault.

89. **Thick and thin:** We've been friends **through thick and thin**.

90. **Ups and downs:** Life is full of **ups and downs**.

91. **Vim and vigour:** He's full of **vim and vigour**.

92. **Wine and dine:** He promised to **wine and dine** me.

93. **X-ray and ultrasound:** The doctor ordered an **X-ray and ultrasound** to diagnose the problem.

94. **Year in, year out: Year in, year out**, we vacation at the same spot.

95. **Zig and zag:** The path would **zig and zag** through the forest.

96. **Above and beyond:** She went **above and beyond** to help her friend.

97. **Bread and circuses:** The government distracts the public with **bread and circuses**.

98. **Cool, calm, and collected:** Despite the pressure, he remained **cool, calm, and collected**.

99. **Down and dirty:** They got **down and dirty** in the mud.

100. **Ends and odds:** I've been sorting through the **ends and odds** in the garage.

101. **Fine and dandy:** Despite the challenges, everything is **fine and dandy**.

102. **High and mighty:** Some people act **high and mighty** when they're in positions of power.

103. **Out and proud:** She's **out and proud**, embracing her true self.

104. **Peachy keen:** Despite the setbacks, he always says he's **peachy keen**.

105. **Quiet and serene:** The mountain lake is a place of **quiet and serene** beauty.

106. **Ripe and ready:** The fruit is **ripe and ready** for harvest.

107. **Sleep and dream:** After a long day, all I want to do is **sleep and dream**.

108. **True and blue:** He's a **true and blue** friend, always there when you need him.

109. **Whistle and hum:** Walking through the forest, all you could hear was the **whistle and hum** of nature.

110. **Xanadu and Beyond:** The explorer ventured into **Xanadu and beyond**, seeking the unknown.

111. **Youth and exuberance:** The project was filled with the **youth and exuberance** of the team.

112. **Zephyr and breeze:** The gentle **zephyr and breeze** rustled through the leaves.

113. **Air and space:** The exhibit showcased the wonders of **air and space** exploration.

114. **Bright and brilliant:** Her ideas were always **bright and brilliant**, illuminating any discussion.

115. **Calm and composed:** In times of crisis, she remained **calm and composed**.

116. **Dusk and dawn:** The magical moments between **dusk and dawn** are truly captivating.

117. **Echo and reverberation:** The canyon echoed with the **reverberation and echo** of their laughter.

118. **Fall and rise:** Life is a journey of constant **fall and rise**, learning and growing.

119. **Glisten and sparkle:** The dew on the grass would **glisten and sparkle** in the morning sun.

120. **Hum and rhythm:** The city had its own **hum and rhythm**, a symphony of urban life.

121. **Ink and parchment:** The author crafted tales with **ink and parchment**, weaving literary magic.

122. **Joy and jubilation:** The announcement was met with **joy and jubilation**.

123. **Kaleidoscope and spectrum:** The festival was a **kaleidoscope of colours and vibrant spectrum**.

124. **Lush and verdant:** The valley was **lush and verdant**, a haven of natural beauty.

125. **Moonlight and shadows:** The garden was bathed in **moonlight and shadows**, casting enchanting shadows.

126. **Nestle and cradle:** The baby is **nestled in the cradle**, peacefully asleep.

127. **Ocean and horizon:** Standing on the beach, the vast **ocean and horizon** met the distant horizon.

128. **Peacock and plumage:** The **peacock and its vibrant plumage** proudly displayed.

129. **Quietude and hush:** The library was a haven of **quietude and hush**, perfect for reading.

130. **Rhythm and rhyme:** The poet played with **rhythm and rhyme** to create lyrical verses.

131. **Starry and celestial:** The **night sky was filled with starry and celestial** wonders.

132. **Twilight and mystery:** The forest took on an air of **twilight and mystery** as the sunset.

133. **Unwind and relax:** After a long day, it's essential to **unwind and relax**.

134. **Vibrant and lively:** The marketplace was **vibrant and lively**, bustling with activity.

135. **Wanderlust and adventure:** The traveller embraced **wanderlust and sought new adventure**

Note: *Binomial pairs are different from phrases and collocations in that they are two words that are always used together and in the same order, connected by a conjunction like "and" or "or". Phrases are groups of words that work together to convey a particular meaning, but they don't necessarily have to be used in a specific order. Collocations are words that often go together, but they can be flexible in terms of order and can be separated by other words.*

Mastering binomial pairs is a key aspect of improving spoken English. They are commonly used in everyday conversation and can make your English sound more natural and fluent. By using binomial pairs correctly, you can express complex ideas more succinctly and clearly. They also add a rhythmic quality to your speech, making it more engaging and pleasant to listen to. So, keep practising these binomial pairs and take your English speaking skills to the next level! Happy learning! ☺

Key 11

Question and Answer Method

Your Shortcut to Fluent English

Understanding how to form and respond to questions is a fundamental aspect of communication, and it plays a crucial role in learning any language, including English. This involves the use of 'Wh-' words, auxiliary verbs like 'do', 'does', 'did', 'be' verbs, and knowing how to answer with 'yes' or 'no' or provide direct answers.

Forming Questions

1. **'Wh-' Words**: 'Wh-' words include "what", "where", "when", "who", "why", "which", and "how". They are used to ask for specific information. For example, "What is your name?", "Where do you live?", "When is the meeting?".

2. **Do, Does, Did**: These auxiliary verbs are used to form questions in the present simple and past simple tenses. For example, "Do you like coffee?", "Does she work here?", "Did you go to the concert?".

3. **Be Verbs:** 'Be' verbs, including "am", "is", "are", "was", and "were", can be used to form questions. For example, "Are you ready?", "Is she your friend?", "Were they at the party?".

4. **Have**: This auxiliary verb is used to form perfect tenses. For example, I have finished my homework, She has gone to the market.

In addition to these, modal auxiliary verbs express necessity, possibility, permission, or ability. These include can, could, may, might, shall, should, will, would, must.

Responding to Questions:

1. **Yes/No Answers**: Some questions can be answered with a simple 'yes' or 'no'. For example, in response to "Do you like coffee?", you can say "Yes, I do" or "No, I don't".

2. **Direct Answers**: 'Wh-' questions usually require more information in the answer. For example, in response to "What is your name?", you would provide your name.

When responding to 'Wh-' questions, you can often replace the 'Wh-' word with the relevant information. Here's how it works:

• For a question like "What is your name?", you replace 'What' with your name. So, if your name is John, your answer would be "John".

•	For "Where do you live?", replace 'Where' with your location. If you live in New York, you would say "New York".

•	For "When is your birthday?", you replace 'When' with the date of your birthday. If your birthday is on January 1st, you would say "January 1st".

This method provides a straightforward way to answer 'Wh-' questions accurately and efficiently. It's a simple yet effective strategy for improving your spoken English. Keep practising, and you'll see improvement in no time! ☺

The Dual Role: Speaker and Listener

In the Q&A method, you play a dual role - you're both the speaker and the listener. This dual role is what makes this method so effective. As the speaker, you're actively constructing sentences and expressing ideas. As the listener, you're processing information, understanding context, and formulating responses

Mastering the art of question and answer can significantly improve your spoken English. It can help you engage in meaningful conversations, express your thoughts and opinions, and understand others better. So, keep practising and happy learning!

Testimony:

- I've tried it, and it really works. You'll become a better English speaker without even noticing.

Key 12

Small Talk

Your Spoken English Sidekick 🗣 ♂

Imagine you're at a party or a social gathering. You see a group of people chatting, and you want to join in Or you're struggling to keep the conversation going? But how do you break the ice? Well, that's where **small talk** comes in. It's like the **masala chai** of conversations - a little bit can add a whole lot of flavour! ☕

What is Small Talk? 🗨

Small talk is the art of engaging in casual and light-hearted conversations, often with people we don't know well. It is a conversation about **everyday matters**. Small talk is the casual, everyday conversation we have with people we know or meet for the first time. It's the **chit-chat that happens before a mee**ting, **in line at the grocery store,** or **while waiting for the bus**. It's a key skill in mastering spoken English, especially for us Indians, as it helps us break the ice and build connections. It's perfectly like the 'masala chai' of conversations - light, refreshing, and perfect for any occasion!

Why is Small Talk Important ? 🎯

Mastering 'Small Talk' can help you:

1. **Break the Ice**: It's a great way to start a conversation.

2. **Build Connections**: It helps you connect with others on a personal level. It shows that you're interested in the other person.

3. **Improve English**: It's a fantastic way to practise and improve your spoken English.

Small Talk Topics 🗣

Here are some common 'Small Talk' topics:

- **Weather**: "It's really hot today, isn't it?"

- **Food**: "Have you tried the new biryani place in town?"

- **Sports**: "Did you catch the cricket match last night?"

- **Food**: Discussing local cuisines, favourite dishes, or recent meals can be a great conversation starter. For example, "Have you tried the new biryani place in town?" 🍲

- **Travel**: Sharing travel experiences or future travel plans can also spark interesting conversations. "Have you visited any interesting places recently?"

- **Hobbies**: Asking about someone's hobbies can help you learn more about their interests. "Do you have any hobbies?" 🎨

- **Work or Study**: Talking about one's profession or field of study can be a good way to understand their background. "What do you do for a living?" or "What are you studying?" 📚

- **Music**: Discussing favourite genres, artists, or concerts can be a fun topic. "Who's your favourite singer?" ♪

Small Talk in Indian Context:

In India, we love our cricket and Bollywood. So, these can be great topics for small talk. For example:

- **Cricket**: "Did you see Kohli's century in the last match?" 🏏

- **Bollywood**: "Have you watched the latest Ranveer Singh movie?" 🎬

Small Talk Tips 📝

1. **Keep it Light**: Small talk is about casual, easy-going topics. Avoid heavy or controversial subjects.

2. **Listen Actively**: Show interest in what the other person is saying.

3. **Ask Open-Ended Questions**: These are questions that can't be answered with a simple 'yes' or 'no'. For example, "What did you think of the movie?"

4. **Start with simple questions.** When you're first getting started, stick to simple questions that are easy to answer. For example, you could ask someone about their day, their job, or their hobbies.

5. **Compliment Them**: A sincere compliment can be a great conversation starter. For example, "That's a nice watch. Where did you get it from?"

6. **Talk About Common Interests**: If you know you have something in common with the other person, bring it up. For example, "I heard you like cricket. Who's your favourite player?"

- **Be Observant**: Use your surroundings to come up with topics. Maybe they're holding a book by an author you like, or they're wearing a t-shirt of a band you listen to.

Use common phrases. Here's a list of common phrases that can be used in small talk:

1. **Greetings**: "Hello! How are you?"
2. **Weather**: "It's a lovely day, isn't it?"
3. **Work**: "How's work going?"
4. **Weekend**: "Got any plans for the weekend?"
5. **Hobbies**: "What do you like to do in your free time?"
6. **Travel**: "Been to any interesting places recently?"
7. **Food**: "Tried any new restaurants lately?"
8. **Movies/TV Shows**: "Seen any good movies or TV shows lately?"
9. **Books**: "Read any good books lately?"
10. **Sports**: "Did you catch the game last night?"

11.   * "How's it going?"

12.   * "What have you been up to?"

13.   * "What do you do for fun?"

14.   * "I love your [article of clothing/accessory]."

15.   * "That's interesting. Tell me more."

What to avoid: avoiding certain mistakes can make your small talk more effective and enjoyable. Here are some common pitfalls to steer clear of:

1. **Avoid Controversial Topics**: Politics, religion, and personal issues can lead to heated discussions. It's best to stick to light and neutral topics.

2. **Don't Monopolize the Conversation**: Small talk is a two-way street. Make sure to listen and show interest in what the other person is saying.

3. **Avoid Close-Ended Questions**: These can kill the conversation as they can be answered with a simple 'yes' or 'no'. Instead, ask open-ended questions that encourage a more detailed response.

4. **Don't Be Too Personal**: Asking overly personal questions can make the other person uncomfortable. Keep the conversation casual and respectful.

Remember, the goal of small talk is to build a connection, so keep it light, respectful, and enjoyable. Happy chatting! ☺Sure, here's a list of common phrases that can be used in small talk:

Key 13

Conversational Connectors

Means for Seamless Dialogue

For new English learners, mastering conversational connectors is a transformative game-changer. These linguistic bridges, like "**By the Way**," "**However**," and "**On the Other Hand**," play a pivotal role in connecting sentences, enabling seamless communication and elevating spoken English.

Understanding the significance of these **connectors** is like unlocking a secret code to fluent and engaging conversations. They act as the **glue** that binds thoughts and ideas, allowing you to traverse the landscape of spoken English with ease. By incorporating these connectors into your language toolkit, you enhance the flow of discussions and cultivate finesse that captivates your audience.

Whether sharing **anecdotes**, expressing **opinion**s, or navigating complex topics, these connectors become **allies, empowering you to speak seamlessly**. They're more than just words; they are keys that unlock the door to articulate and confident communication. Embrace the **importance** of conversational connectors, and watch how they become the **game-changer** in your journey to master spoken English

1. "By the Way": The Subtle Segue

Example: *Original Sentence:* "I love exploring new cultures. The food in Italy is incredible."

Enhanced with Connector: "I love exploring new cultures. By the way, the food in Italy is incredible."

"By the way" effortlessly introduces a related point, enriching the conversation without interrupting its natural rhythm.

2. "However": Navigating Contrasts

Example: *Original Sentence:* "The weather forecast predicted rain. We decided to go for a hike."

Enhanced with Connector: "The weather forecast predicted rain. However, we decided to go for a hike."

"However" smoothly introduces a contrast, allowing for a nuanced expression of opposing ideas.

3. "On the Other Hand": Balancing Perspectives

Example: *Original Sentence:* "Studying abroad is exciting. It can also be challenging."

Enhanced with Connector: "Studying abroad is exciting. On the other hand, it can also be challenging."

"On the other hand" introduces an alternative viewpoint, fostering a balanced and comprehensive conversation.

4. Linking Words: Enhancing Coherence

Example: *Original Sentences:* "I enjoy reading. I also like hiking."

Enhanced with Linking Words: "I enjoy reading; moreover, I also like hiking."

Linking words like "moreover" enhances coherence, creating a smoother transition between related ideas.

5. "In Addition": AmpingUp Information

Example: *Original Sentence:* "I have a passion for painting. I love photography as well."

Enhanced with Connector: "I have a passion for painting. In addition, I love photography."

"In addition" adds depth by signalling the addition of complementary information.

6. "Therefore": Drawing Logical Conclusions

Example: *Original Sentence:* "She worked hard on her project. She achieved great results."

Enhanced with Connector: "She worked hard on her project. Therefore, she achieved great results."

"Therefore" establishes a logical connection, highlighting a cause-and-effect relationship between ideas.

In Conclusion: Conversational connectors are the invisible threads that weave your spoken words into a coherent tapestry. Whether you're subtly shifting topics, contrasting ideas, or adding layers to your narrative, these connectors enhance the fluency and impact of your spoken English. Practice incorporating them into your conversations, and witness how they transform mere words into a captivating dialogue. Let us go-

1. **Adding Information:**
   - Moreover
   - Furthermore
   - In addition
   - Additionally
   - Besides

2. **Showing Contrast:**
   - However
   - On the other hand
   - Nevertheless
   - Nonetheless
   - But
   - Yet

3. **Introducing Examples:**
   - For example
   - For instance
   - Such as
   - Namely

4. **Sequencing Ideas:**

- Firstly
- Secondly
- Lastly
- Finally
- Next
- Then

5. **Expressing Similarity:**
   - Similarly
   - Likewise
   - In the same way

6. **Concluding or Summarizing:**
   - In conclusion
   - To sum up
   - Overall
   - To summarize
   - All in all

7. **Emphasizing Points:**
   - Indeed
   - In fact
   - Certainly
   - Undoubtedly

8. **Time Sequence:**
   - Meanwhile
   - Simultaneously
   - Subsequently
   - Consequently

9. **Clarifying or Reinforcing:**
   - That is to say
   - In other words
   - To clarify

- I mean
- Specifically

10. **Contrasting Ideas:**
    - While
    - Whereas
    - Unlike
    - On the contrary

11. **Expressing Cause and Effect:**
    - Therefore
    - Thus
    - Hence
    - Consequently
    - As a result

12. **Agreeing with a Point:**
    - I agree
    - Exactly
    - Absolutely
    - Definitely
    - That's true

13. **Disagreeing with a Point:**
    - I disagree
    - On the contrary
    - Not necessarily
    - However, I think...

14. **Expressing Conditions:**
    - If
    - Unless
    - Provided that
    - In case

15. **Expressing Purpose:**

- So that
- In order to
- With the aim of
- For the purpose of

Remember to use these connectors appropriately based on the context of your conversation. Practice incorporating them whenever necessary.

Just imagine you like to continue or lengthen your sentence coherently(logically), conversational connectors can work for you / or come to your help/assistance.

<u>Practice Sheet:</u>

1. *I woke up late morning. ____, I missed the bus to work.*
2. *She loves to travel; her passion has taken her to many countries. ____, she enjoys immersing herself in different cultures.*
3. *The weather was unpredictable. ____, we decided to have a picnic in the park.*
4. *I have a meeting at 2 pm. ____, I need to prepare the presentation.*
5. *I'm going to the store. ____, I'll pick up some groceries on the way home.*
6. *He was tired after a long day at work. ____, he still went to the gym for a workout.*
7. *I love reading novels. ____, I can spend hours lost in a good book.*

Key No 14

Common Social Expressions

Every language has some fixed Expressions which are used on particular social occasions. English does not have very many expressions of this kind. Whether introducing yourself, extending a holiday greeting, or expressing gratitude, knowing the correct phrases to use can make all the difference.

Here you get a range of expressions for each occasion-from greetings and farewells to special occasions and everyday interactions. So, get ready to improve your English communication skills with these common fixed expressions. Happy learning! ☺

Introductions:
- "Hello, my name is..."
- "I'd like to introduce myself. I'm..."
- "Pleased to meet you."
- "Allow me to introduce myself."
- "I don't think we've met before, I'm..."

Greetings:
- "Good morning/afternoon/evening."

- "How's it going?"
- "Hi, how are you?"
- "Hey, good to see you!"
- "Hello, how's your day going?"

Asking about health:
- "How are you feeling?"
- "Are you feeling better?"
- "How have you been keeping?"
- "I hope you're feeling well."
- "Are you okay?"

Special greetings:
- "Happy birthday!"
- "Congratulations on your promotion!"
- "Best wishes on your wedding!"
- "Good luck with your exam!"

Holidays:
- "Merry Christmas!"
- "Happy New Year!"
- "Happy Easter!"
- "Happy Thanksgiving!"
- "Have a great holiday!"

Journeys:
- "Have a safe journey."
- "Enjoy your trip."
- "Wishing you a fantastic trip."
- "Hope you have a great time."
- "Looking forward to hearing about your travels."

Meals:
- "Enjoy your meal."

- "Would you like seconds?"
- "Bon appétit!"
- "Hope you enjoy your food."
- "This looks delicious, doesn't it?"

Visits and Invitations:
- "Would you like to come over for dinner?"
- "It was nice having you over."
- "It's always a pleasure to have you over."
- "You're always welcome at our place."
- "We should do this again sometime."

Sleep:
- "Sleep well."
- "Sweet dreams."
- "Have a good night."
- "Hope you get a good rest."
- "Sleep tight."

Giving things:
- "Here you go."
- "This is for you."
- "This is a small token for you."
- "I thought you might like this."
- "I got this for you."

Asking for things:
- "Could I borrow your pen, please?"
- "May I have a glass of water?"
- "Could you please pass the salt?"
- "May I use your phone?"

- "Could I have a moment of your time?"

Thanks:

- "Thank you very much."
- "I really appreciate it."
- "I can't thank you enough."
- "I'm really grateful."
- "Your help is much appreciated."

Remember, these phrases are often used in specific contexts and may vary based on the relationship between the speakers. Happy learning! ☺

Key 15

Stress/Accent

(Have you)Ever wondered why the word 'PHO-to-graph' transforms into 'pho-TOG-ra-phy' when we say 'photography'? Or why the sentence "I DIDN'T say you stole the money" sounds different from "I didn't SAY you stole the money"? Welcome to the fascinating world of 'stress' in spoken English!

Stress, in the realm of spoken English, is a fascinating concept that adds rhythm and melody to our speech. It's not about tension or anxiety, but about giving prominence, the emphasis we place on certain syllables or words when we speak. It's the heartbeat of the language, giving life to our words and clarity to our sentences.

The Power of Stress

Stress is like the secret sauce that can change the flavour of a word. For instance, consider the word 'present'. If we stress the first syllable, it becomes 'PRE-sent', **a noun meaning a gift.** But if we stress the second syllable, it transforms into 'pre-SENT', a **verb meaning to introduce**. The same word, but different meanings, all thanks to stress!

Let's get deeper with more examples. Here are some words where the meaning changes based on which **syllable** we stress:

1. 'CON-tract' (a legal agreement) vs 'con-TRACT' (to shrink)
2. 'IN-sult' (to offend) vs 'in-SULT' (offensive remark)
3. 'OB-ject' (a thing) vs 'ob-JECT' (to disagree)
4. 'PER-fect' (flawless) vs 'per-FECT' (to improve)
5. 'REB-el' (a person who resists authority) vs 're-BEL' (to resist authority)
6. 'REC-ord' (a disc that music is recorded on) vs 're-CORD' (to store sound or pictures, usually on discs or tapes)
7. 'REF-use' (garbage) vs 're-FUSE' (to decline)
8. 'SUB-ject' (a topic) vs 'sub-JECT' (to make somebody/something experience, suffer or be affected by something, usually unpleasant)
9. 'SUS-pect' (a person thought to be guilty of a crime) vs 'sus-PECT' (to think that something is probably true)

Misplacing the stress can lead to confusion or even miscommunication. That's why getting the stress right is so important!

Stress and Its Siblings: Accent and Emphasis

While stress is about the emphasis within a word, 'accent' is about the unique way a group of people pronounce a word. It's like the regional flavour added to the language. For example, the way we Indians roll our 'R's or stretch our 'A's, that's our Indian English accent! **Accent** is essentially the stress laid upon a syllable in pronouncing a word. Therefore, in every word, there can be a primary accent (the syllable that is pronounced with the greatest force) and a secondary accent (the syllable that is pronounced with less force but more than the unaccented syllables).

On the other hand, **'emphasis'** is about highlighting a word in a sentence. It's like using a highlighter pen on our speech. For example, "I DIDN'T say you stole the money" places emphasis on the speaker's denial, whereas "I didn't SAY you stole the money" implies that someone else made the accusation. **Given its utmost relevance in spoken English, we will explore emphasis in more detail in a separate section.**
Some tips to remember:

- Most two-syllable nouns and adjectives have the stress on the first syllable, such as "HAP-py", "TA-ble", and "WA-ter".

- Most two-syllable verbs have the stress on the second syllable, such as "re-LAX", "de-CIDE", and "be-GIN".

- Some prefixes and suffixes do not affect the stress of the word, such as "un-HAP-py", "re-LAX-ed", and "be-GIN-ner".

- Some prefixes and suffixes change the stress of the word, such as "pho-TO-graph", "pho-TO-graph-er", and "pho-TO-graph-ic".

The Magic of Stress

In conclusion, stress is like the magic wand that can transform our spoken English. It **adds rhythm, clarifies meaning,** and makes our speech more **engaging and understandable.** So, let's learn this delightful key and put the right 'stress' on our pronunciation. After all, English is not just a language, it's a symphony of sounds

---

Let's Use this space:

English is described as a '**rhythm-bound and stress-timed'** language, that relies heavily on the **concept of stress'**. This means that the rhythm of English is like music with a steady beat. The 'beat' or 'stress' is the extra force that you give to certain words or parts of words when you speak.

Some Sentences with Stress:

1. The an**cient** oak tree, with its gnarled branches stretching towards the hea**vens**, became a sym**bol** of en**dur**ing strength and re**sil**ience for the com**mu**nity.

2. In the heart of the bus**tling** mar**ket**, the vi**brant** stalls adorned with an ar**ray** of ex**otic** spi**ces** and tex**tiles** created a ka**lei**do**scope** of co**lours**, en**ticing** pas**ser**sby with their al**lure**.

Key 16

Intonation

At its core, intonation is the rise and fall of the pitch in your voice as you speak. It's the musicality of your speech, adding a dynamic layer beyond just the words. Imagine you're at a play. The actors are delivering their lines, but something **feels off**. They're speaking in a **monotone**, with *no variation in pitch or tone*. The dialogue feels flat and **lifeless**, right? This is exactly what happens when we don't use intonation in our speech.

Types of Intonation

There are three main types of intonation in English:

1. **Rising Intonation:**

   - **Description:** The pitch of your voice rises towards the end of a sentence.

- **Common Usage:** Often used in yes/no questions, indicating curiosity or seeking confirmation.

- **Example:** "You're coming to the party, aren't you?"

2. **Falling Intonation:**

- **Description:** The pitch drops towards the end of a sentence.

- **Common Usage:** This is when the pitch of the voice decreases with time. It's commonly used in statements or wh-questions (who, what, where, etc.). For example, in the sentence "I live in Delhi.", the pitch falls at the end, indicating a statement.

- **Example:** "I really enjoyed the movie."

3. **Fall-Rise Intonation:**

- **Description:** A combination of falling and rising pitch, creating a nuanced tone. Starts with a rise and ends with a fall, often conveying surprise or strong emotion.

- **Common Usage:** This is a combination of the above two. The pitch falls first and then rises. It's often used to express uncertainty or when the speaker is not sure. For example, "Maybe." The pitch falls on 'may-' and rises on '-be', indicating uncertainty.

- **Example:** "You could give me a hand with this, perhaps?", "You did WHAT?!"

Why is Intonation Important?

Let's take an example. Say the phrase "Really?" in a surprised tone. Now, say it in a sarcastic tone. Notice the difference? That's intonation at work! It changes the meaning of the phrase entirely.

In English, intonation is crucial. It helps us understand the speaker's attitude and intentions. It can turn a statement into a question, show surprise, indicate doubt, and much more.

How Can Intonation Help Indian Learners?

For Indian learners, mastering intonation can be a game-changer. Here's why:

1. **Clarity**: English is a stress-timed language. This means some syllables are longer, and some are shorter. By using intonation, your speech becomes clearer and easier to understand.

2. **Fluency**: With correct intonation, your English sounds more natural and fluent. You'll sound more like a native speaker.

3. **Expression**: Intonation allows you to express emotions and attitudes. It brings your speech to life, making it more engaging and impactful.

How to Improve Your Intonation?

Here are some tips to improve your intonation:

1. **Listen and Repeat**: Listen to native English speakers. Pay attention to their intonation. Try repeating what they say and match their tone.

2. **Record Yourself**: Record your speech and listen to it. Notice the areas where your intonation is off.

3. **Practice**: Like any other skill, practice makes perfect. Read aloud and try to use intonation. Practice with different types of sentences - statements, questions, exclamations.

Remember, intonation is a powerful tool in spoken English. It's like the spice in a dish. Without it, the dish is bland (tasteless). But with it, the dish comes to life. So, let's start practising and add some spice to our English-speaking skills!

It's the subtle yet powerful art that transforms your language skills from good to exceptional, making your conversations more enjoyable, relatable, and impactful. So, embrace the rise and fall, dance with the pitch, and let intonation be the melody of your spoken English journey.

Food for thought.

Intonation is the music of language. It's the rise and fall of our voice when we speak. It's not about what we say, but how we say it. Intonation gives emotion, meaning, and context to our words.

Key 17

Emphasis: Fine-tuning Spoken English

Have you ever noticed how some speakers *captivate you with their words*? They seem to have a magic wand(**baton**) that makes their speech more engaging. That magic wand is 'Emphasis'.

What is Emphasis?

Emphasis is the strength given to words or phrases that makes them stand out in a sentence. It's like highlighting text in a book. You're drawing attention to specific information. Emphasis is a key aspect of spoken English that can help you effectively convey your message and capture the listener's attention. By placing emphasis on certain words, phrases, or even sentences, you can highlight important information and add emotion or emphasis to your speech.

Ways to Achieve Emphasis

There are several ways to achieve emphasis in spoken English:

1. **Stress. (Volume)**: One way to emphasize words in spoken English is by using **stress**. This involves pronouncing certain words or syllables with more

force or prominence. For example, in the sentence "I really **love** chocolate," you can emphasize the word "love" to convey strong feelings about chocolate.

2. **Pitch**: Another way to add emphasis is through **intonation**. This refers to the rise and fall of your voice as you speak. By using a rising intonation, you can indicate that a question is being asked, while a falling intonation can signal the end of a statement. For example, "I didn't take the **last** piece of cake."

3. **Pausing**: A pause before or after a word can emphasize it. For example, "I am... excited."

4. **Speed**: Speaking a word more slowly can give it more emphasis. For example, "You are u-n-b-e-l-i-e-v-a-b-l-e."

5. **Repetition**: Repeating a word or phrase also gives it more emphasis. For example, "I really, really like it."

Why is Emphasis Important?

Emphasis changes the meaning of a sentence. For example, consider the sentence "I didn't say he stole the money." This sentence has seven different meanings, depending on which word you emphasize:

1. **I** didn't say he stole the money - Someone else said it.

2. I **didn't** say he stole the money - I'm denying it.

3. I didn't **say** he stole the money - I implied it.

4. I didn't say **he** stole the money - I said someone else did.

5. I didn't say he **stole** the money - Maybe he just borrowed it.

6. I didn't say he stole **the** money - He stole some money, just not that money.

7. I didn't say he stole the **money** - He stole something else.

See how the meaning changes with emphasis?

Additionally, using **pauses** can also help to emphasize certain words or phrases. By pausing before or after a keyword, you can draw attention to it and give it more importance in the sentence.

Example:

- Sentence: "I didn't say you stole my money."

  Emphasising different words shifts the meaning:

1. I didn't say **you** stole my money. (Someone else did.)

2. I didn't say you **stole** my money. (But maybe you did something else.)

3. I didn't say you stole **my** money. (It could be someone else's money.)

4.   I didn't say you stole my **money**. (You might have taken something else.)

Mastering emphasis takes practice. Pay attention to how native speakers use stress, intonation, and pauses. Practice in different contexts and notice how it changes your speech's meaning.

By mastering emphasis in spoken English, you can effectively communicate your message, capture your listener's attention, and convey emotions and attitudes in your speech. Keep practising and experimenting with emphasis to become a confident and engaging speaker in English.

Let's have some examples: Practise Emphasis on different words:

- The **ancient** oak tree, with its gnarled branches stretching towards the heavens, became a symbol of enduring strength and resilience for the community.

- The ancient **oak tree**, with its gnarled branches stretching towards the heavens, became **a symbol** of enduring strength and resilience for the community.

- The ancient oak tree, with its gnarled branches stretching towards the heavens, became a symbol of **enduring strength and resilience** for the community.

Key 18

Pauses

The Secret Sauce of Clear and Impactful Speaking

Let's talk about something often overlooked but seriously **powerful** in spoken English – **pauses**. Think of them as the **quiet moments** between your words, and they're more important than you might realize.

1. Like Punctuation in Sentences:

Pauses in speaking are a bit like the **commas and periods** in writing. They help **organize** your thoughts and guide your listeners. It's like a **dance**, and **pauses** are the cool moves that make your speech smooth and easy to follow.

2. Building Suspense:

Imagine telling a story without a **pause** before the big reveal. **Pauses** build **suspense**. They make people **pay attention**, and curious about what you're going to say next. It's like the **quiet before a surprise**, making your words more **interesting**.

3. Making Words Stand Out:

Ever notice how a good joke has **perfect timing**? **Pauses** do that. They make certain words or ideas stand out, like turning on a **spotlight**. Your audience gets to really get what you're saying, and it makes your message **stick**.

4. Helping People Understand:

Pauses are like little breaks in your speech. They help your listeners **understand** what you're saying. It's like taking a **breath** between sentences – it gives everyone a chance to **catch up** and keeps things **clear**.

5. Showing How You Feel:
Ever heard someone speak with **feeling**? It's often because of **pauses**. A **pause** can show **hesitation, excitement, or deep thinking**. It's like adding **emotion** to your words, making your English sound more **real** and **natural**.

6. Taking Your Time to Think: When you **pause**, it shows you're **thinking** about what you want to say. It's like taking a moment to **pick the right words**, and that **thoughtfulness** makes your speech sound more **put together**.

So, the next time you're talking, remember the **power** of **pauses**. They're not just gaps in your words; they're the secret ingredient that makes your speaking **clear, interesting**, and full of **emotion**. Use them well, and watch your spoken English become a smooth and impactful conversation.

Key 19

Tone of Voice

Tone of Voice in Spoken English

Have you ever wondered why some people sound more confident, friendly, or persuasive when they speak English? Have you ever felt frustrated or misunderstood when you try to express yourself in English? Have you ever wished you could speak English more naturally and fluently?

If you answered yes to any of these questions, then this article is for you. In this article, you will learn about one of the most important aspects of spoken English that can make a huge difference in your communication: your tone of voice.

What is tone of voice and why is it important?

Tone of voice is the way you use your voice to convey your emotions, attitude, and personality. It is not just about what you say, but how you say it. Tone of voice can make a big difference in how your message is received and understood by others.

For example, imagine you are saying the same sentence in different situations:

- "I'm sorry." (You accidentally bumped into someone on the street)

- "I'm sorry." (You forgot to do your homework and your teacher is angry)

- "I'm sorry." (You broke up with your partner and you regret it)

Can you hear how your tone of voice would change in each scenario? You would probably use a different pitch, volume, speed, and intonation to express your feelings and intentions.

Tone of voice is especially important for Indian learners of English because it can help you overcome some of the challenges that you may face, such as:

- **Accent**: You may have a strong regional or native accent that makes it hard for others to understand you. By using the right tone of voice, you can emphasize the keywords and phrases, and make your speech more clear and comprehensible.

- **Vocabulary:** You may not have a large or varied vocabulary that allows you to express yourself precisely and accurately. By using the right tone of voice, you can add more meaning and nuance to your words, and make your speech more rich and interesting.

- **Culture**: You may not be familiar with the cultural norms and expectations of the English-speaking world. By using the right tone of voice, you can show respect, politeness, and friendliness, and make your speech more appropriate and acceptable.

What are the different types of tone of voice and how to use them?

There are many different types of tone of voice that you can use in spoken English, depending on the situation, the purpose, and the audience. Here are some of the most common ones and how to use them with examples:

- **Neutral:** This is the most basic and common tone of voice that you can use in most situations. It is neither too high nor too low, neither too loud nor too soft, neither too fast nor too slow, neither too flat nor too varied. It is calm, clear, and professional. You can use this tone of voice when you want to be informative, factual, or objective. For example:

  o "The capital of India is New Delhi."

  o "The weather today is sunny and warm."

  o "The meeting will start at 10 a.m."

- **Positive**: This is a tone of voice that you can use when you want to be friendly, enthusiastic, or optimistic. It is slightly higher, louder, faster, and more varied than the neutral tone. It is cheerful, lively, and energetic. You can use this tone of voice when you want to show interest, appreciation, or agreement. For example:

o "I'm so happy to see you!"

o "That's a great idea!"

o "I agree with you completely!"

- **Negative:** This is a tone of voice that you can use when you want to be angry, sad, or pessimistic. It is slightly lower, softer, slower, and less varied than the neutral tone. It is dull, gloomy, and tense. You can use this tone of voice when you want to show disappointment, dissatisfaction, or disagreement. For example:

o "I'm so sorry to hear that."

o "That's a terrible idea!"

o "I disagree with you completely!"

- **Questioning**: This is a tone of voice that you can use when you want to ask a question, seek clarification, or express doubt. It is usually higher, louder, faster, and more varied than the neutral tone. It is curious, inquisitive, and uncertain. You can use this tone of voice when you want to show curiosity, confusion, or hesitation. For example:

o "What did you say?"

o "Are you sure about that?"

o "How do you know that?"

- **Commanding:** This is a tone of voice that you can use when you want to give an order, make a request, or express urgency. It is usually lower, louder, faster, and less varied than the neutral tone. It is firm, assertive, and confident. You can use this tone of voice when you want to show authority, responsibility, or importance. For example:

  o "Stop that right now!"

  o "Please do this for me."

  o "We need to hurry up!"

How to play with tone of voice and semantics?

Semantics is the study of the *meaning of words and sentences*. By playing with tone of voice and semantics, you can create different effects and impressions in your spoken English. You can use tone of voice to change the meaning of the same words or sentences or to emphasize the meaning of different words or sentences. Here are some examples of how you can play with tone of voice and semantics:

- **Sarcasm**: This is when you use a tone of voice that is opposite to the literal meaning of the words or sentences, to express irony, mockery, or contempt. For example:

  o "Wow, you're so smart." (You think the person is stupid)

- o "That's very funny." (You think the person is not funny at all)
- o "I'm so happy for you." (You think the person is not happy at all)
- **Humour**: This is when you use a tone of voice that is unexpected or **exaggerated**, to express amusement, laughter, or fun. For example:
  - o "I love Mondays." (You hate Mondays)
  - o "That's the best thing I've ever heard." (You think the thing is ridiculous or boring)
  - o "You're such a good friend." (You think the person is a bad friend)
- **Irony:** This is when you use a tone of voice that is contrary to reality or expectation, to express surprise, disappointment, or criticism. For example:
  - o "What a beautiful day." (The day is rainy and cold)
  - o "That's exactly what I wanted." (You wanted something else)
  - o "You're so helpful." (You think the person is not helpful at all)

How to improve your tone of voice in spoken English?

The best way to improve your tone of voice in spoken English is to practice it as much as possible. Here are some tips that you can try:

- **Listen and copy**: Listen to how Amitabh Bachchan speaks in his movies. Try to copy his tone.
- **Record and check**: Record yourself saying "I love biryani." Listen to it. Can you make it sound more exciting?

- **Try different tones**: Say "It's raining" in a happy tone, a sad tone, and a surprised tone. See how it changes the meaning?

Here are some types of tone of voice and examples:

1. **Happy Tone**: Your voice is lively and the pitch goes up. For example, "What a wonderful day!"

2. **Sad Tone**: Your voice is slower and softer. For example, "I miss my friends."

3. **Angry Tone**: Your voice is loud and fast. For example, "I can't believe this!"

4. **Surprised Tone**: Your voice is high-pitched and quick. For example, "Wow, I didn't expect that!"

5. **Confused Tone**: Your voice is hesitant and the pitch goes up at the end. For example, "I don't understand this?"

6. **Serious Tone**: Your voice is steady and calm. For example, "We need to talk about this."

7. **Motivating Tone**: Your voice is enthusiastic and encouraging. For example, "You can do it! I believe in you!"

8. **Respectful Tone**: Your voice is polite and shows admiration. For example, "I really appreciate your help."

Conclusion

Tone of voice is a powerful tool that can help you enhance your spoken English and make it more effective and engaging. By paying attention to your tone of voice, you can express yourself better, understand others better, and connect with them better. **So, what are you waiting for? Start working on your tone of voice today and see the difference it makes!**

Key 20

Question Tags/ Tag Questions

Hello, language explorer! 🙋‍♀️ Want to make your English conversations more engaging? Let's unlock the secret of 'Question Tags'. They're like the 'chaat masala' of English - a pinch can transform a simple sentence into a tangy conversation! 🌶️

1. What are Question Tags?

Picture this: you're telling a friend, "This movie is interesting." Add a twist at the end: "This movie is interesting, isn't it?" Voila! You've just used a question tag - "isn't it?" So, Question tags are short questions that are added to the end of a statement. They are used to confirm information, to check if someone agrees with you, or to ask for more information. For example, "You like coffee, don't you?" or "It's a beautiful day, isn't it?"

Question tags convert statements into questions. They're a fantastic tool to engage your listener, verify information, or keep the conversation going.

2. Why are Question Tags important?

Question tags are an essential part of spoken English. They help you sound more natural and engaging in conversations. They also help you to keep the conversation going by encouraging the other person to respond.

3. The Rule of Opposites

Question tags follow the rule of opposites. If your statement is positive, the question tag is negative. For example, "She's a good singer, isn't she?" And vice versa: "He isn't coming to the meeting, is he?"

4. The Indian Touch

As Indian speakers, we sometimes use question tags in our unique way, like "We're late, no?" While it adds a desi flavour, remember that in formal or international settings, it's better to stick to standard forms like "aren't we?"

5. How to use Question Tags?

To use a question tag, you need to identify the auxiliary verb in the statement. If there is **no auxiliary verb,** you can use the **verb "do**". For example, "You like coffee, don't you?" or "She is a doctor, isn't she?".

Tips for using Question Tags:

- Use question tags to confirm information or to check if someone agrees with you.

- Use rising intonation when asking a question tag.

- Use the correct auxiliary verb in the question tag.

- Use negative question tags to show surprise or disbelief.

- Use positive question tags to show agreement or to encourage a response

Examples of Question Tags:
- You're coming to the party, aren't you?
- She's a great singer, isn't she?
- He doesn't like pizza, does he?
- You haven't seen the movie yet, have you?
- We're going to the beach, aren't we?
- "The weather is nice today, isn't it?"
- "You didn't forget the meeting, did you?"
- "She can play the guitar, can't she?"
- "We haven't met before, have we?"

Now, let's explore two more types of questions: Appended Questions and Indirect (Reported) Questions.

****Appended Questions**** are like the surprise guests at a party. They appear at the end of a statement or another question, adding an extra layer of inquiry or confirmation.

For instance, consider the sentence, **"You're going to the party, right?" Here, "right?"** is an appended question that seeks confirmation about the preceding statement.

On the other hand, **Indirect (Reported) Questions** are the messengers of the question world. They don't ask the question directly, but instead, they relay a question asked by someone else. The structure of these questions is more like a statement, and there's no inversion of word order. For example, "**He asked me what was wrong**." Here, the direct question "**What's wrong?**" is reported indirectly.

While Tag Questions, Appended Questions, and Indirect Questions can all be used to seek confirmation or additional information, they differ in their structure and usage. Tag questions are used at the end of a statement to ask for confirmation or agreement, appended questions are added to the end of a statement or question, and indirect questions report a question asked by someone else. So, next time you're in a conversation, see if you can spot these different types of questions! It's a fun way to become more aware of how we communicate.

I hope this helps you master spoken English. Remember to practise using question tags in your conversations to become more fluent and confident. Happy learning! 🚀

Remember:

So, start using question tags in your English conversations and see the magic unfold. Happy chatting! 🎉

Practice Sheet: Add Question Tag

1. You enjoy learning new languages......................
2. She has been to Paris before......................
3. We're going to the concert tonight......................
4. He doesn't like spicy food......................
5. They have finished their homework......................
6. It's a beautiful day......................
7. You wouldn't mind helping......................
8. She won't forget to call......................
9. They've never been to Asia......................
10. We can meet at the usual place......................
11. He's a talented musician......................
12. You haven't seen that movie......................
13. She always arrives on time......................
14. You don't mind waiting for a moment......................

Add anything you like:

KEY 21

Power of Adjectives and Adverbs

Spicing Up Your Language

You know, even though we're not diving into an **English Grammar book** here, I've got to tell you - having a **good handle on adjectives and adverbs** can make a **language sing/ workable**. It's like being **a chef and knowing just the right spices to add to your dish**. It can turn **a bland** (tasteless) conversation into something flavourful and memorable. So, let's chat about these **"spices" of language, shall we?**

Adjectives and adverbs are words that modify or describe other words, such as nouns, pronouns, and verbs. They can make our spoken English more precise, expressive, and interesting. For example, instead of saying "She is a teacher", we can say "She is a **dedicated** teacher" or "She is a teacher **who loves her students**". The adjectives 'dedicated' and 'who loves her students' give more information about the noun 'teacher'. Similarly, instead of saying "He runs fast", we can say "He runs **very** fast" or "He runs **faster than anyone else**". The adverbs 'very' and '**faster than anyone else**' modify the verb 'runs' and show the degree or comparison of the action.

Knowledge of **adjectives and adverbs** can help us improve our spoken English in many ways. Some of them are:

- We can use **adjectives and adverbs** to compare and contrast things or people. For example, "This book is **more interesting** than that one" or "She sings **better** than him".
- We can use **adjectives and adverbs** to express our opinions, feelings, or attitudes. For example, "I am **happy** that you are here" or "He is **really annoying** me".
- We can use **adjectives and adverbs** to emphasize or modify our statements. For example, "She is **extremely smart**" or "He **hardly ever** studies".
- We can use **adjectives and adverbs** to add variety and richness to our vocabulary. For example, "The sky is **blue**" or "The sky is **azure**".

Therefore, knowledge of **adjectives and adverbs** is essential for improving our spoken English. We cannot avoid using them in our day-to-day conversation in English. They can help us communicate more effectively and creatively with others

Here are some examples of different types of adjectives through some conversational pieces with Indian names:

- **Proper adjectives** are adjectives that are derived from proper nouns, such as names of people, places, or things.

They are usually capitalized and modify common nouns. For example:

o Priya: I love **Italian** food. It's so delicious and varied.
o Ravi: Me too. What's your favourite **Italian** dish?
o Priya: I like **Neapolitan** pizza and **Tuscan** pasta. How about you?
o Ravi: I prefer **Sicilian** seafood and **Roman** gelato.

In this conversation, the words in bold are proper adjectives. They tell us the origin or style of the food or dish.

- **Descriptive adjectives** are adjectives that describe the quality or characteristic of a noun or pronoun. They can be positive or negative and can express subjective or objective opinions. For example:
    - o Anjali: You look **beautiful** today. I like your **red** dress.
    - o Rohit: Thank you. You are very **kind**. I like your **blue** shirt.
    - o Anjali: Thanks. It's **new**. I bought it yesterday.
    - o Rohit: It suits you. You have **good** taste in clothes.

In this conversation, the words in bold are descriptive adjectives. They tell us how Anjali and Rohit look, feel, or act, and what colour or condition their clothes are.

- **Quantitative adjectives** are adjectives that indicate the quantity or amount of a noun or pronoun. They can be exact or approximate and can be expressed in numbers or words. For example:

- o   Raj: How **many** books do you have?
- o   Meera: I have **three** books. How **much** money do you have?
- o   Raj: I have **twenty** rupees. How **many** cookies do you want?
- o   Meera: I want **some** cookies. How **much** milk do you need?

In this conversation, the words in bold are quantitative adjectives. They tell us how many books, money, or cookies Raj and Meera have or want, and how much money or milk they have or need.

- **Demonstrative adjectives** are adjectives that point out or identify a specific noun or pronoun. They include **this, that, these**, and **those**. For example:
  - o   Amit: Do you like **this** movie?
  - o   Nisha: No, I don't. I prefer **that** one.
  - o   Amit: Why? What's wrong with **this** one?
  - o   Nisha: It's too boring. **That** one is more exciting.

In this conversation, the words in bold are demonstrative adjectives. They tell us which movie Amit and Nisha are talking about or watching.

- **Distributive adjectives** are adjectives that indicate that something is distributed or divided among the members of a group. They include **each**, **every**, **either**, **neither**, and **any**. For example:

- Sam: We have **four** pizzas. How should we divide them?
- Pam: Let's give **each** person a slice of **every** pizza.
- Sam: That sounds fair. Do you want **either** of the drinks?
- Pam: No, thanks. I like **neither** of them. I'll have **any** of the desserts.

In this conversation, the words in bold are distributive adjectives. They tell us how the pizzas, drinks, and desserts are distributed or chosen by Sam and Pam.

- **Interrogative adjectives** are adjectives that are used to ask questions about a noun or pronoun. They include **what**, **which**, and **whose**. For example:
  - Arjun: **What** book are you reading?
  - Neha: I'm reading **this** book. It's very interesting.
  - Arjun: **Which** book is it? I can't see the title.
  - Neha: It's **this** one. It's called "The Mystery of the Missing Diamond".
  - Arjun: **Whose** book is it? Is it yours or someone else's?
  - Neha: It's mine. I bought it yesterday.

In this conversation, the words in bold are interrogative adjectives. They tell us what Arjun wants to know about Neha's book.

- **Possessive adjectives** are adjectives that show ownership or possession of a noun or pronoun. They include **my**, **your**, **his**, **her**, **its**, **our**, and **their**. For example:
  - Rani: Is this **your** dog?
  - Raju: Yes, it is. He's **my** dog. His name is Moti.
  - Rani: He's very cute. What's **his** breed?
  - Raju: He's a mixed breed. He has **his** mother's ears and **his** father's tail.
  - Rani: Where are **they** now?
  - Raju: They are at **my** house. They are **my** pets too.

Numeral adjectives are adjectives that indicate the order or position of a noun or pronoun in a series. They include ordinal numbers (such as **first**, **second**, **third**, etc.) and multiplicative numbers (such as **once**, **twice**, **thrice**, etc.). For example:

- Priya: I'm going to the library. Do you want to come with me?
- Ravi: Sure. What are you going to do there?
- Priya: I'm going to borrow some books. I need them for my project.
- Ravi: How **many** books do you need?
- Priya: I need **five** books. I have a list of them here.

- Ravi: Let me see. The **first** book is "The History of Ancient Rome". The **second** book is "The Art of War". The **third** book is "The Rise and Fall of the Roman Empire". The **fourth** book is "The Life of Julius Caesar". The **fifth** book is "The Legacy of Rome".
- Priya: That's right. You have a good memory. You only saw the list **once**.
- Ravi: Thank you. I try to remember things I see or hear **twice** or **thrice**.

You can also look for it because it is useful:

Compound Adjectives:

Definition: These adjectives are formed by combining two or more words to create a hyphenated phrase that modifies a noun.

- Examples:
- The team had a **last-minute** strategy change.
- She wore a **red-and-white** dress to the party.
- It was a **well-written** novel.

Let us understand **Averbs** through examples because **examples are better than precepts**:

Adverbs of Frequency are adverbs that indicate how often an action or event happens. They include words like always, never, often, sometimes, rarely, etc. For example:

- Priya: Do you **always** go to the temple in the morning?

- o Ravi: No, I **usually** go in the evening. But today I had a meeting, so I went in the morning.
- o Priya: I see. I **never** go to the temple. I prefer to meditate at home.
- o Ravi: Really? How **often** do you meditate at home?
- o Priya: I try to meditate **every day**, but **sometimes** I skip a day or two.
- o

2. **Adverbs of Degree** are adverbs that indicate how much, how little, or to what extent something is true. They include words like very, too, extremely, quite, enough, etc. For example:
    - o Neha: How was the movie?
    - o Arjun: It was **very** good. I enjoyed it a lot.
    - o Neha: Really? I heard it was **too** long and boring.
    - o Arjun: No, it wasn't. It was **quite** interesting and engaging.
    - o Neha: Well, maybe I'll watch it then. Is it **enough** to buy a ticket online, or do I need to book a seat?

In this conversation, the words in bold are adverbs of degree. They tell us how good, long, interesting, or necessary the movie or the ticket is.

3. **Adverbs of Manner** are adverbs that indicate how something is done or happens. They usually end with -ly, but there are some exceptions. They

include words like quickly, slowly, carefully, loudly, etc. For example:

- o Anjali: How did you finish the project so **quickly**?
- o Rohit: I worked **hard** and **efficiently**. I didn't waste any time.
- o Anjali: Wow, that's impressive. I worked **slowly** and **carefully**. I wanted to make sure everything was perfect.
- o Rohit: That's good too. But you shouldn't work **too hard**. You need to relax **sometimes**.

In this conversation, the words in bold are adverbs of manner. They tell us how Anjali and Rohit finished the project, worked, or relaxed.

4. **Adverbs of Place** are adverbs that indicate where something is or happens. They include words like here, there, everywhere, nowhere, etc. For example:
    - o Raj: Where are you going?
    - o Meera: I'm going to the market.
    - o Raj: Why are you going **there**?
    - o Meera: Because I need to buy some vegetables.
    - o Raj: Can't you buy them **here**?
    - o Meera: No, it's too expensive **here**. I need a cheaper place.
    - o Raj: Well, good luck. I'll see you **later**.

In this conversation, the words in bold are adverbs of place. They tell us where Raj and Meera are going, buying, or seeing each other.

5. **Adverbs of time** are adverbs that indicate when something happens or how long it lasts. They include words like now, then, soon, yesterday, today, tomorrow, etc. For example:
    - Amit: When are you leaving for the airport?
    - Nisha: I'm leaving **now**. My flight is in two hours.
    - Amit: Oh, **then** you should hurry. The traffic is bad at this time of the day.
    - Nisha: I know. That's why I booked a cab in advance. It should be **here soon**.
    - Amit: OK, good. Have a safe trip. I'll miss you.
    - Nisha: I'll miss you too. I'll call you **tomorrow** when I arrive.

Adjectives to Adverbs: Now, let's get into another angle on how adjectives can, in most cases, be transformed into adverbs. The process involved in making this transformation is neither tricky nor puzzling. In fact, it's a simple trick that can significantly boost the count of your vocabulary stock.

Adjectives are words that describe or modify other words, typically nouns. For example, in the phrase "a **beautiful** sunset", 'beautiful' is an adjective that describes the noun 'sunset'.

The magic happens when we add the suffix '**-ly**' to an adjective, transforming it into an **adverb**. Adverbs are words that modify verbs, adjectives, or other adverbs. They often tell us how, when, where, or to what extent something happens.

Take our adjective 'beautiful'. By adding '-ly', we get '**beautifully**', an adverb. So, instead of saying "She sings in a beautiful way", we can say "She sings **beautifully**". Notice how the sentence becomes more concise and elegant?

This transformation isn't limited to 'beautiful'. It works with many adjectives! '**Quick**' becomes '**quickly**', '**happy**' becomes '**happily**', '**loud**' becomes '**loudly**', and so on. Each time you do this, you're effectively adding a new word to your vocabulary.

However, keep in mind that not all adjectives can be turned into adverbs by adding '-ly', and not all words ending in '-ly' are adverbs. English is full of exceptions! For example, '**friendly**' is an adjective, not an adverb. To express the adverbial sense of 'friendly', we would say "in a friendly way".

In addition to the '-ly' rule, there are other ways to form adverbs from adjectives:

- Some adjectives and adverbs have the same form. For example, '**fast**' is both an adjective and an adverb. You can say "He is a **fast** runner" (adjective) and "He runs **fast**" (adverb).

- Some adjectives add '**-wise**' to become adverbs. For example, '**clockwise**', '**otherwise**', and '**likewise**'.
- Some adjectives change completely to become adverbs. For example, 'good' becomes 'well', and 'late' becomes 'lately'.

So,   start **experimenting** with **adjectives** and **adverbs** in your conversations. You'll find that your language becomes more vibrant, precise, and expressive. Happy learning!

Improve the sentences: by adding Adjectives and adverbs:

1.   The cat sat on the chair.
2.   She walked through the park.
3.   The flowers bloomed in the garden.
4.   He spoke at the conference.
5.   The sun set behind the mountains.

Answer:

1. The cat sat on the **comfortable, upholstered** chair.
2. She walked through the **serenely beautiful** park.
3. The **vividly coloured** flowers bloomed in the **meticulously tended** garden.
4. He spoke **eloquently** at the conference.
5. The sun set behind the **majestic, snow-capped** mountains.

Key 22

Body Language/ Gestures

Do you want to speak English like a native speaker? Do you want to impress your listeners with your fluency, clarity, and confidence? Do you want to avoid misunderstandings and express yourself better? If you answered yes to any of these questions, then you need to pay attention to one thing: your body language and gestures.

Body language and gestures are non-verbal ways of communicating your thoughts, feelings, and attitudes through your facial expressions, eye contact, hand movements, body posture, and voice tone. They are essential for speaking English because they can enhance your words, show your emotions, and convey your intentions. In fact, research shows that body language and gestures account for more than 50% of the meaning of a message, while words only account for 7%.

Another reason why body language and gestures are important in spoken English is that they are natural and inevitable. Any speech is communicated with the body of the human being, especially the organs of speech, such as the mouth, tongue, teeth, and throat. Hence, body language and gestures are always part of your speech, whether you are aware of them or not. They can make your speech more natural and authentic, or they can make it unnatural and artificial, depending on how you use them.

In this article, we will show you why body language and gestures are one master key to improving your spoken English, and how you can use them effectively.

Why are body language and gestures important in spoken English?

Body language and gestures are important in spoken English for several reasons, such as:

- They can add variety, emphasis, and complexity to your sentences by using inversions, which are when you change the normal word order of a sentence by putting the verb before the subject. For example, instead of saying "You are very kind", you can use an inversion and say "Very kind you are". This makes your sentence sound more interesting and expressive. You can also use your facial expressions and gestures to show your appreciation and gratitude.
- They can show disapproval, annoyance, scepticism, or contrast by using negative adverbs or adverb phrases, such as never, rarely, hardly, etc. rolling your eyes, shaking your head, or using air quotes. For example, if someone says "I never lie" and rolls their eyes, they are probably implying that they lie a lot. You can also use your voice tone and intonation to show your sarcasm and irony.

- They can avoid misunderstandings by using facial expressions, eye contact, and gestures that match your words and tone. For example, if you say "I'm sorry" with a sincere smile and a nod, you will sound more genuine and apologetic than if you say it with a frown and a shrug. You can also use your eye contact and gestures to show your interest and attention to the speaker and to signal when you want to speak or listen.
- They can appear confident and interested by using a straight posture, open shoulders, nodding, smiling, and gesturing with their hands. These body language cues can also help you breathe more fully and speak more clearly. You can also use your voice volume and speed to show your confidence and enthusiasm.

How can you use body language and gestures effectively in spoken English?

To use body language and gestures effectively in spoken English, you need to:

- Observe how native speakers use them in different situations, such as podcasts, videos, books, or websites. You can also learn from online resources, such as apps, websites, or blogs, that teach you about body language and gestures in English.
- Practice using them in your speech, by recording yourself and listening to your voice, or by speaking with native speakers or other learners. You can also use speech-

to-text apps to check your pronunciation or get direct feedback from a tutor, a friend, or yourself.

• Experiment with different body language and gestures, and see how they affect your speech and understanding. You can also try to guess the meaning and intention of other people's body language and gestures and compare them with your own

Body language and gestures are one master key to improving your spoken English because they can help you communicate more effectively, clearly, and confidently. They can also help you understand the meaning and intention of other people's words, especially when they use sarcasm, irony, humour, or idioms. To use body language and gestures effectively in spoken English, you need to observe, practice, and experiment with them. We hope this article helps you improve your spoken English. If you have any questions or comments, please feel free to ask us. We are always happy to help you. ☺

Speculate the following and ponder:

1. **Job Interview:**
• In what ways can body language and gestures convey confidence and professionalism during a job interview?
2. **Public Speaking:**
• How can expressive gestures and body language enhance the impact of a public speech or presentation?
3. **Negotiation:**
• What specific body language cues can be employed to foster a positive atmosphere and successful negotiation?

Key 23

Four Pillers of Speech

The Art of Conversation

So, you're on a journey to master English conversations, aren't you? Whether it's English, Assamese, or any other language, the essence of a good conversation remains the same. Well, let me tell you, It's not just about the words we use, but how we use them to express ourselves and understand others.

But here's the thing, real-life conversations can be tricky. They don't always follow a set pattern and can sometimes take unexpected turns. They can deviate, move away from the expected, and become ambiguous. The way a person speaks during a conversation can vary greatly depending on their personality, mood, and the context of the conversation.

But don't worry, I've got some insider tips for you. These are the Four Pillars, the unspoken rules that form the basis of cooperative conversation. **Intrigued/sound interested**? Let's dive in!

One way to ensure *effective communication* is by following the ***Four Pillars, the kind of maxims that form the basis***

of cooperative conversation. They are the unspoken rules or Key Principles for Cooperative Dialogue.

1. Don't Overdo It (Quantity)

Share just enough information, not too much or too little. You don't want to confuse or bore the other person!

- Example: If someone asks where you live, "I live in Delhi" is enough. No need for your full address!

2. Be Honest (Quality)

Tell the truth. If you don't know something, it's okay to say so.

- Example: Don't know the answer to a question? Just say, "I'm not sure about that."

3. Stay on Topic (Relevance)

Keep your comments related to the conversation. Going off on a tangent can be confusing.

- Example: If you're talking about cricket, don't suddenly start talking about cooking.

4. Keep It Clear (Manner)

Be clear and to the point. Avoid being vague or overly wordy.

- Example: Say "the glass," not "the thing you use to drink that's round and made of glass."

Understanding and applying these principles can significantly improve your conversational skills in English. They help in making the conversation more cooperative and meaningful. So, the next time you're in a conversation, remember these unspoken rules and see the difference they make!

Remember, practice and real-world application are the keys to mastering English conversation. So, keep practising, and you'll surely make great strides in your English learning journey! Happy conversation! 🗣

Things to ponder:

Our main goal here is to improve our English speaking skills. And to do that effectively, cooperative conversation is a must. It's not just about knowing the language but also about how we use it to communicate and connect with others. So, let's embrace these Four Pillars of conversation and make our English communication more effective and engaging. Remember, "Master the art of conversation, and you'll have the world listening to you. Let's make every conversation count!" 🗣

Practice Sheet:

- Q: "How many siblings do you have?"
- A: "Some."
- Violation: The answer provides insufficient information, violating the maxim of quantity.

- Q: "Did you finish the report?"
- A: "Of course, it's a masterpiece."
- Violation: The answer includes an exaggerated claim, violating the maxim of quality.
- Q: "What's your favourite book genre?"
- A: "I recently painted my room blue."
- Violation: The answer is unrelated to the question, violating the maxim of relation.
- Q: "Can you explain the scientific method?"
- A: "It's like, you know, a bunch of steps and stuff."
- Violation: The answer is vague and lacks clarity, violating the maxim of manner.

- Q: "Have you been to Paris?"
- A: "Well, last summer was crazy. I lost my sunglasses, and the food was so-so. Oh, and I met this interesting guy."
- Violation: The answer not only fails to directly answer the question (violation of relation) but also includes unnecessary information (violation of quantity) and lacks precision (violation of manner).

Practice:

Key 24

Variety of/in Expressions

Variety is the spice of life- **William Cowper**

(Have you) Ever thought about how you can say the same thing in different ways? Understanding spoken English can be tricky due to the many expressions used in different situations. This diversity is what makes English interesting. Want to learn how to express ideas in various ways in English? Do you want to know how to choose the right words for different situations and audiences? If yes, then it's time to explore the variety of expressions in English.

Expressing yourself differently is the ability to use various forms and styles of language to communicate effectively. It makes spoken English more appealing, clear, and convincing. It also helps avoid repeating the same thing, causing confusion or boredom. So, are you ready to learn the variety of expressions in spoken English? If yes, let's start.

Let's see how we can use variety in expressions and what it means in English.

Active and Passive Voice(s)

One way to use variety in expression is to switch between active and passive voice. Active voice is when the subject of the sentence acts. Passive voice is when the subject of the sentence receives the action. For example:

- Active voice: She wrote a letter. (She is the subject and the doer of the action.)

- Passive voice: A letter was written by her. (A letter is the subject and the receiver of the action.)

Some tips to remember:

- Active voice is usually more direct, concise, and lively. It is preferred for most situations, especially when you want to emphasize the agent or the actor of the action. For example: "I love you." or "He broke the window."

- Passive voice is usually more indirect, wordy, and formal. It is preferred for some situations, especially when you want to emphasize the patient or the object of the action, or when the agent or the actor is unknown, irrelevant, or obvious. For example: "The results were announced." or "The window was broken."

Polite and formal language

Another way to use variety in expression is to choose between polite and formal language. Polite language is when you use words and phrases that show respect, courtesy, and consideration for others. Formal language is when you use words and phrases that follow the rules and conventions of standard English. For example:

- Polite language: Could you please pass me the salt? (Could is a modal verb that shows a request.)

- Formal language: Would you mind passing me the salt? (Would is a modal verb that shows a conditional.)

Some tips to remember:

- Polite language is usually more friendly, casual, and conversational. It is preferred for most situations, especially when you want to build rapport, show appreciation, or make suggestions. For example: "Thank you for your help." or "How about we go to the movies?"

- Formal language is usually more serious, professional, and academic. It is preferred for some situations, especially when you want to show authority, accuracy, or distance. For example: "We appreciate your assistance." or "It is suggested that we attend the cinema."

Simple and complex sentences

A third way to use variety in expression is to mix simple and complex sentences. Simple sentences are sentences that have only one independent clause. Complex sentences have one independent clause and one or more dependent clauses. For example:

- Simple sentence: She likes chocolate. (She likes chocolate is an independent clause that can stand alone as a complete sentence.)

- Complex sentence: She likes chocolate because it makes her happy. (She likes chocolate is an independent clause and because it makes her happy is a dependent clause that cannot stand alone as a complete sentence.)

Some tips to remember:

- Simple sentences are usually more clear, easy, and short. They are preferred for most situations, especially when you want to state facts, give commands, or create impact. For example: "The sky is blue." or "Stop it." or "Wow."

- Complex sentences are usually more detailed, difficult, and long. They are preferred for some situations, especially when you want to explain reasons, show relationships, or add information. For example: "The sky is blue because of the way sunlight is scattered by the atmosphere." or "Stop it or I will call the police." or "Wow, that was amazing."

Expanding and substituting words

A fourth way to use variety in expression is to expand and substitute words. Expanding words is when you add more words to make your message more descriptive, specific, or persuasive. Substituting words is when you replace words with synonyms or antonyms to make your message more diverse, accurate, or interesting. For example:

- Expanding words: She is happy. -> She is extremely happy. (Extremely is an adverb that modifies the adjective happy.)

- Substituting words: She is happy. -> She is delighted. (Delighted is a synonym of happy.)

Some tips to remember:

- Expanding words is usually more effective, expressive, and convincing. It is preferred for most situations, especially when you want to emphasize, illustrate, or persuade. For example: "He is a good friend." -> "He is a loyal, supportive, and generous friend."

- Substituting words is usually more varied, precise, and creative. It is preferred for some situations, especially when you want to avoid repetition, clarify, or impress. For example: "He is a good friend." -> "He is a splendid companion."

Using One-word substitution

One-word substitution is a skill that can help you achieve a variety of expressions in spoken English. One-word substitution is when you use one word to replace a longer or more complex phrase in English. For example, you can say "ambidextrous" instead of "able to use both hands equally well". One-word substitution can help you make your spoken English more concise, precise, and interesting. It can also help you avoid repetition, confusion, and boredom. If you practice one-word substitution, you can improve your spoken English as an Indian student.

However, you should use one-word substitution only when you know that your listener can understand it. Otherwise, **it is preferable to use a phrase that explains the meaning**

clearly. For example, if your listener is not familiar with the word "philanthropist", you can say **"a person who helps the poor and needy"** instead. This way, you can make sure that your message is clear and effective.

Let's apply a variety of/in Expressions:

Take the sentence "I am happy.":

1. **Casual Conversation**: In a casual setting, you might say, "I'm stoked!" or "I'm over the moon!" These phrases are more informal and often used among friends.

2. **Formal Setting**: In a more formal context, such as a business meeting or an academic conference, you might say, "I am pleased" or "I am content." These expressions are more reserved and professional.

3. **Written Communication:** In writing, especially in a literary context, you could say, "I am engulfed in joy" or "Happiness has taken hold of me." "I am brimming with joy" or "Happiness has enveloped me." These phrases are more descriptive and evoke vivid imagery.

4. **Regional Variations**: Colloquial expressions can also come into play depending on where you are in the world. For example, in Australia, you might hear **"I'm chuffed,"** while in the United States, you might hear **"I'm psyched."**

5. **Indian English Variations**: English is often mixed with local languages in India, leading to unique expressions. For example, you might hear "I'm full happy," a direct translation from several Indian languages.

Remember, context is key when choosing how to express yourself. By understanding these variations, learners can unlock the ability to comprehend and engage in diverse conversational settings, enhancing their mastery of spoken English.

Let us look for more examples:

We can express the same idea. Here are your examples:

1. Expressing happiness:

   - "I am happy."
   - "I am contented."
   - "I am thrilled."

Each of these sentences conveys the feeling of happiness but with varying degrees of intensity. "Thrilled" often implies a higher level of excitement than "happy" or "contented."

2. Asking someone to come tomorrow:

   - "Can you come tomorrow?"
   - "Will you come tomorrow?"

Both sentences ask someone to come tomorrow, but the first is a request, while the second is more of a question about the person's plans.

3. Expressing agreement:

   - "I agree with you."
   - "You're absolutely right."
   - "I couldn't agree more."
   - "That's a good point."

Each of these sentences conveys agreement but with varying degrees of emphasis.

4. Asking about someone's well-being:

- "How are you?"
- "How's it going?"
- "How have you been?"
- "What's up?"

All these questions are used to ask about someone's well-being, but they vary in formality and context.

5. Expressing gratitude:

- "Thank you."
- "I appreciate it."
- "That's very kind of you."
- "I'm grateful."

These sentences all express gratitude, but they can be used in different situations and carry slightly different connotations.

6. Making a suggestion:

- "Let's go to the park."
- "How about going to the park?"
- "We could go to the park."
- "What if we go to the park?"

These sentences all suggest the same activity, but they do so in different ways.

Remember, the variety in expression not only adds richness to the language but also allows us to convey subtle differences in meaning, tone, and context. Understanding these variations can greatly enhance your mastery of English. Keep practising! 👍

Attention:

As you can see, variety in expression is a very important and valuable skill in English. By learning how to use different forms and styles of language, you can master your spoken English and communicate better and more confidently. ☺

As a beginner, you can adopt/ use any one of the above varieties given whenever/ wherever necessary. The fact is you have to speak in any of the ways:

■ As you continue on the journey through these pages, take a moment to recalibrate—a verbal journey unfolding with each exchange, marking milestones in our shared exploration of ideas.

In this reflective pause, savour the collaborative nature of our verbal journey. Appreciate the progress made, the insights gained, and the connections formed through our shared exploration.

Now, as you flip through these pages, anticipate a magical shift. Brace yourself, for we are about to delve into a **world of enchanting verbs,** each holding the power to transform our dialogue into a linguistic adventure.

Key 25

Commonly used Verbs

Do you want to speak English better? Do you want to say what you want to say in any situation? If yes, then you need to learn how to use some of the most common and useful verbs in English: have, get, do, make, and play.

These verbs are very good because you can use them in many different ways. They can help you talk about many things, such as what you do every day, what you like to do, what you plan to do, what you have done, and more. They can also help you make different kinds of sentences, such as questions, negatives, and past, present, and future.

I consider them the "**most beautiful and versatile verbs**" because they effortlessly improve the fluidity of conversations. You can be ready to supercharge your English skills and add a dash of excitement to your conversations. Let's we'll explore some commonly used verbs that work like **magic when paired with specific nouns**. So, let's buckle up and discover how verbs like 'have,' 'make,' 'take,' 'do,' 'give,' 'play,' and 'go' can bring your English to life! These versatile verbs **wield the power to connect thoughts and actions in a way that makes spoken English a delightful experience.**

Let's take a look at each of these verbs and see how they can improve your spoken English.

"**Have**": This word is a versatile companion, pairing seamlessly with various nouns. "Have a rest," "have a cup of tea," or "Have your bathe" showcase its adaptability, making conversations smooth and expressive.

"**Make**": The artistry of "make" adds a creative touch to spoken English. Whether it's "make mistakes," "make a

cake," or "make progress," this verb transforms mundane actions into vibrant expressions.

"**Do**": The simplicity of "do" makes it a linguistic workhorse. "Do business," "do the laundry," or "do a favour" encapsulate its ability to encapsulate diverse activities with a single word.

"Take": "Take" brings a sense of ownership and action. "Take measures," "take a break," or "take a chance" illustrate how this verb elevates conversations by encapsulating various actions

."Get": The dynamic nature of "get" adds energy to spoken English. "Get ready," "get to know," or "get a job" showcase its adaptability in capturing diverse situations.

I firmly believe that with these words, one can pass an entire day of conversation. "Have a great morning," "have a cup of tea," "have a rest," or "have your lunch" — each use of "have" paints a different hue on the canvas of daily interaction, offering a versatile tool for expression.

[Once a learner starts knowing and using these verbs with certain other nouns or words, he will discover a new dimension in his fluency in English. It will be like 'something has always been handy but you have neither used nor focused. These verbs, once you learn, can change the conversational pace and supply the shortage of your word stock.]

Can we have the above verbs with certain nouns:

Expressions with Verb "Have:

Here are some common phrases and expressions with the verb 'have' followed by a noun:

1. Have a rest

2. Have a look

3. Have a try

4. Have a go

5. Have a drink

6. Have a meal

7. Have a chat

8. Have a laugh

9. Have a cry

10. Have a dance

11. Have a read

12. Have a walk

13. Have a run

14. Have a drive

15. Have a ride

16. Have a trip

17. Have a holiday

18. Have a vacation

19. Have a party

20. Have a celebration

21. Have a meeting
22. Have a conference
23. Have a debate
24. Have a discussion
25. Have a fight
26. Have a match
27. Have a competition
28. Have a race
29. Have a battle
30. Have a war
31. Have a good day
32. Have a bath
33. Have a cup of tea

34. Have an idea
35. Have a thought
36. Have a plan
37. Have a goal
38. Have a dream
39. Have a nightmare
40. Have a wish
41. Have a hope
42. Have a fear
43. Have a doubt
44. Have a question
45. Have an answer
46. Have a problem

47. Have a solution
48. Have a suggestion
49. Have a complaint
50. Have a comment

Expressions with Verb "Make':

Here are some common phrases and expressions with the verb 'make' followed by a noun:

1. Make a decision
2. Make a difference
3. Make a discovery
4. Make a fortune
5. Make a fuss
6. Make a journey
7. Make a mistake
8. Make a noise
9. Make a plan
10. Make a promise
11. Make a speech
12. Make a suggestion
13. Make an effort
14. Make an excuse
15. Make an impression
16. Make an observation
17. Make an offer
18. Make peace
19. Make progress
20. Make room
21. Make sense
22. Make time
23. Make trouble
24. Make way

25.   Make a change
26.   Make a choice
27.   Make a comment
28.   Make a contribution
29.   Make a demand
30.   Make a prediction
31.   Make a reservation
32.   Make a statement
33.   Make a visit
34.   Make an announcement
35.   Make an appointment
36.   Make an argument
37.   Make an arrangement
38.   Make an assumption
39.   Make an attempt
40.   Make an inquiry
41.   Make an investment
42.   Make an invitation
43.   Make an order
44.   Make an organization
45.   Make a payment
46.   Make a phone call
47.   Make a prediction
48.   Make a promise
49.   Make a proposal
50.   Make a profit

Expressions with Verb "Take'

1.   Take a break
2.   Take a seat
3.   Take a walk
4.   Take a nap
5.   Take a shower

6. Take a picture
7. Take a test
8. Take a chance
9. Take a look
10. Take a turn
11. Take a step
12. Take a sip
13. Take a bite
14. Take a breath
15. Take a stand
16. Take a vacation
17. Take a leave
18. Take a class
19. Take a course
20. Take a flight
21. Take a trip
22. Take a taxi
23. Take a bus
24. Take a train
25. Take a boat
26. Take a drive
27. Take a ride
28. Take a lead
29. Take a loss
30. Take a risk
31. Take a responsibility
32. Take a decision
33. Take a charge
34. Take a toll
35. Take a blame

36. Take a compliment
37. Take a criticism
38. Take a note
39. Take a message
40. Take a measurement
41. Take a temperature
42. Take a pulse
43. Take a blood
44. Take a sample
45. Take a survey
46. Take a rest
47. Take a medicine
48. Take an account
49. Take notice of

Take a

Expressions with the Verb "Do'

Here are some common phrases and expressions with the verb 'do' followed by a noun:

1. Do a favour
2. Do homework
3. Do the dishes
4. Do the laundry
5. Do the shopping
6. Do the cooking
7. Do the cleaning
8. Do a job
9. Do business
10. Do a project
11. Do research

12. Do a report
13. Do a presentation
14. Do a course
15. Do a degree
16. Do an experiment
17. Do exercise
18. Do yoga
19. Do damage
20. Do good
21. Do harm
22. Do a dance
23. Do a drawing
24. Do a painting
25. Do a crossword
26. Do a puzzle
27. Do a quiz
28. Do a task
29. Do a trick
30. Do a survey
31. Do a review
32. Do a check
33. Do a test
34. Do a favour
35. Do a performance
36. Do a play
37. Do a service
38. Do a disservice
39. Do a calculation
40. Do a budget
41. Do a revision

42. Do a rehearsal
43. Do a translation
44. Do a transcription
45. Do a list
46. Do a comparison
47. Do a measurement
48. Do a prediction
49. Do a printout
50. Do a backup

Expressions with the Verb "Give'

1.   Give a call
2.   Give a lecture
3.   Give a presentation
4.   Give a speech
5.   Give a performance
6.   Give a demonstration
7.   Give a response
8.   Give a party
9.   Give a gift
10. Give a compliment
11. Give a discount
12. Give a refund
13. Give a warning
14. Give a signal
15. Give a command
16. Give a try
17. Give a shout
18. Give a hint

19. Give a hand
20. Give a push
21. Give a pull
22. Give a ride
23. Give a wave
24. Give a smile
25. Give a laugh
26. Give a sigh
27. Give a nod
28. Give a look
29. Give a start
30. Give a cheer
31. Give a yell
32. Give a whisper
33. Give a glance
34. Give a stare
35. Give a roar
36. Give a shriek
37. Give a howl
38. Give a moan
39. Give a gasp
40. Give a sob
41. Give a chuckle
42. Give a snort
43. Give a whimper
44. Give a growl
45. Give a squeal
46. Give a hoot
47. Give a grunt
48. Give a groan

49. Give a murmur
50. Give a scream

Phrases with the verb 'Play"

1. Play a game
2. Play a match
3. Play a role
4. Play a part
5. Play a trick
6. Play a joke
7. Play a record
8. Play a song
9. Play a tune
10. Play a melody
11. Play a solo
12. Play a character
13. Play a scene
14. Play a round (as in golf)
15. Play a set (as in tennis)
16. Play a hand (as in cards)

17. Play a move (as in chess)
18. Play a note (as in music)
19. Play a chord (as in music)
20. Play a gig
21. Play a concert
22. Play a show
23. Play a prank
24. Play a sport

25. Play a position (as in team sports)
26. Play a strategy
27. Play a tactic
28. Play a card
29. Play a shot (as in photography or sports)
30. Play a video
31. Play a movie
32. Play a clip
33. Play a track
34. Play a beat
35. Play a rhythm
36. Play a riff
37. Play a sequence
38. Play a level (as in video games)
39. Play a campaign (as in video games)
40. Play a role-play
41. Play a simulation
42. Play a game of chance
43. Play a game of skill
44. Play a round of applause
45. Play a fanfare
46. Play a symphony
47. Play a sonnet
48. Play a suite
49. Play a movement
50. Play a piece

Phrases or Expressions with the verb" Go'

Go + [noun]

1. Go home
2. Go shopping

Go + to + [noun]

1. Go to school
2. Go to work
3. Go to college

Go + to+ the +noun

4. Go to the movies
5. Go to the gym
6. Go to the library
7. Go to the store
8. Go to the mall
9. Go to the beach
10. Go to the airport
11. Go to the station
12. Go to the post office
13. Go to the hospital
14. Go to the doctor
15. Go to the dentist
16. Go to the vet
17. Go to the market
18. Go to the city
19. Go to the country
20. Go to the mountains
21. Go to the sea
22. Go to the lake
23. Go to the river
24. Go to the island
25. Go to the desert
26. Go to the forest

27. Go to the jungle
28. Go to the zoo
29. Go to the museum
30. Go to the art gallery
31. Go to the concert
32. Go to the theatre
33. Go to the opera
34. Go to the ballet
35. Go to the circus
36. Go to the amusement park
37. Go to the water park
38. Go to the aquarium
39. Go to the planetarium
40. Go to the observatory
41. Go to the botanical garden
42. Go to the farm
43. Go to the ranch
44. Go to the vineyard

Go + on + [noun]

1. Go on holiday
2. Go on a trip

With the verb ' Get'

1. **Get Achievement**
2. **Get Understanding**
3. **Get Approval**
4. **Get Access**

5. **Get Attention**
6. **Get Response**
7. **Get Permission**
8. **Get Advantage**
9. **Get Result**
10. **Get Information**
11. **Get Recognition**
12. **Get Support**
13. **Get Solution**
14. **Get Clearance**
15. **Get Completion**
16. **Get Experience**
17. **Get Commencement**
18. **Get Realization**
19. **Get Change**
20. **Get Improvement**
21. **Get Connection**
22. **Get Participation**
23. **Get Completion**
24. **Get Impact**
25. **Get Promotion**

They are different from Collocations?

You might wonder if these phrases are the same as collocations, which are also common combinations of words in English. **The answer is no**, they are not. Collocations are words that usually go together or sound natural together, such as fast food, heavy rain, or making a decision. They are not necessarily verbs and nouns, they can be other parts of speech, such as adjectives and nouns, verbs and adverbs, or nouns and prepositions. Collocations are not fixed or grammatical rules, they are just patterns or habits of the language. (A separate Note is given on **Collocations-Key 9)**. The phrases we are talking about are different from collocations, because they are based on the meanings and uses of the verbs, not on how they sound together. They are also more flexible and variable because you can change the nouns or add other words to modify them, such as have a nice day, have a cup of tea, have a quick shower, have a heated discussion, have a short break, and so on. These phrases are not just combinations of words, they are expressions of ideas and actions.

Mind it: In the realm of spoken English, these verbs act as linguistic bridges, connecting thoughts and actions with elegance. They simplify conversations, adding a touch of beauty to everyday interactions. So, let's celebrate the beauty of "have," "make," "do," "take," and "get" as the essential elements that make passing a day in conversation not just easy but wonderfully expressive.

Key 26

Silent Letters

Silent letters in English words can be quite a puzzle, don't you think? I mean, just look at the word **"knight."** Why on earth is there a "k" at the beginning if we're not supposed to say it? English is full of these intriguing quirks, and silent letters are just one example of the delightful chaos that makes the language so fascinating.

Okay, so here's the lowdown on silent letters: In English, a silent letter is a letter that appears in a particular word, but it's not pronounced when you say the word out loud. It's like a sneaky little ninja hiding in the word, making things a bit more interesting (or confusing) for learners.

Now, why should a learner of English bother mastering these silent letters? Well, let me tell you, understanding silent letters is like uncovering a secret code to fluent spoken English. When you know about silent letters, you can navigate spoken English with more confidence and accuracy. It's like having a special decoder ring that helps you unlock the pronunciation of tricky words.

Let's dive into why knowing silent letters is so crucial for spoken English mastery:

1. Improved Pronunciation

When you know which **letters are silent** in certain words, you can pronounce those words correctly. This is crucial for effective communication because mispronouncing words can lead to misunderstandings. Plus, nailing the pronunciation makes you sound more polished and fluent.

2. Enhanced Listening Skills

Recognizing and understanding silent letters also sharpens your listening skills. As you become more familiar with these hidden letters, you'll start picking them out when others speak. This allows you to grasp spoken English more accurately, which is essential for effective communication, especially in fast-paced conversations.

3. Expanded Vocabulary

Understanding silent letters opens the door to a wider vocabulary. Once you've mastered the silent letters, you'll confidently tackle words that might have previously stumped you. This gives you access to a broader range of words to express yourself, making your spoken English more colourful and expressive.

4. Boosted Confidence

Finally, mastering silent letters can do wonders for your confidence when speaking English. You'll feel more assured in your ability to use the language, and that kind of confidence shines through in conversations. When you're confident in your pronunciation and comprehension, you can express **yourself more fluently and connect with others more effectively**.

In a nutshell, knowing about silent letters is like having a **backstage pass** to the English language. It's a gateway to smoother communication, clearer pronunciation, and a deeper appreciation for the quirks and charms of English.

So, go ahead and embrace the silent letters—uncover their mysteries, practice their pronunciation, and watch as your spoken English skills soar to new heights! And remember, it's all part of the delightful adventure of mastering this wonderfully perplexing language.

Let us have a list of commonly used words in English that contain silent letters. Understanding and practising the pronunciation of these words can be incredibly helpful for mastering spoken English.

Words with Silent "K":
1. Know - /noʊ/ (not /knoʊ/)
2. Knife - /naɪf/ (not /knaɪf/)
3. Knit - /nɪt/ (not /kniːt/)
4. Knee - /niː/ (not /kniː/)

Words with Silent "G":
1. Gnome - /noʊm/ (not /gnoʊm/)
2. Gnat - /næt/ (not /gnæt/)

Words with Silent "H":
1. Hour - /aʊər/ (not /haʊər/)

2. Heir - /ɛər/ (not /hɛər/)

Words with Silent "W":

1. Wreath - /riːθ/ (not /wriːθ/)

2. Wrist - /rɪst/ (not /wrɪst/)

Words with Silent "B":

1. Comb - /koʊm/ (not /koʊmb/)

2. Lamb - /læm/ (not /læmb/)

Words with Silent "L":

1. Talk - /tɔːk/ (not /tɔːlk/)

2. Walk - /wɔːk/ (not /wɔːlk/)

Words with Silent "T":

1. Castle - /ˈkæsl/ (not /ˈkæstəl/)

2. Fasten - /ˈfæsən/ (not /ˈfæstən/)

Words with Silent "P":

1. Pneumonia - /njuːˈmoʊniə/ (not /pəˈnjuːmoʊniə/)

2. Psychology - /saɪˈkɒlədʒi/ (not /saɪˈkɒlədʒi/)

Words with Silent "E":

1. Cute - /kjuːt/ (not /kjuːtɛ/)

2. Surname - /ˈsɜːrneɪm/ (not /ˈsɜːrnəme/)

Words with Silent "R":

1. February - /ˈfɛbruəri/ (not /ˈfɛbruəri/)

2. Colonel - /ˈkɜːrnəl/ (not /ˈkɜːrənəl/)

Understanding and becoming familiar with these words will give you a great head start in mastering the pronunciation and comprehension of English. It's like having a secret map to navigate the twists and turns of the English language.

Here's a list of more words with silent letters:

(Remember these words. It will help your pronunciation)

1. **Words with Silent B**: Aplomb, Bomb, Climb, Comb, Crumb, Debt, Doubt, Dumb, Jamb, Lamb, Limb, Numb, Plumb, Subtle, Succumb, Thumb, Tomb, Womb.

2. **Words with Silent C**: Abscess, Ascend, Ascent, Conscience, Conscious, Crescent, Descend, Disciple, Evanesce, Fascinate, Fluorescent, Muscle, Obscene, Resuscitate, Scenario, Scene, Scissors.

3. **Words with Silent D**: Bridge, Edge, Handkerchief, Handsome, Handful, Grandson, Ledger, Sandwich, Wednesday.

4. **Words with Silent E**: Plaque, Vegetable, Bridge, Clothes, Hate, Name, Like, Breathe.

5. **Words with Silent G**: Align, Assign, Benign, Champagne, Cologne, Consign, Design, Feign, Foreign, Gnarly, Gnash, Gnat, Gnaw, Gnome, Gnomic, High, Light, Reign, Resign, Sign.

Can you FIND OUT some words that contain Silent letters?------

Key 27

Everyday Foreign Words and Phrases

Ever heard someone say "**bonjour**" instead of hello or "**ciao**" instead of goodbye? That's the **magic** of **Key 27**. It's like a **secret code** unlocking a world of words from different places.

Imagine your words becoming little **messengers** that carry bits of other **cultures**. That's what happens when we use **foreign phrases** in our chats. It's not just about **speaking**; it's about **connecting** with people from all over.

From **déjà vu** making you feel like you've seen something before to saying "**fiesta**" when it's time to **party**, these **phrases** are like cool **stickers** you add to your **language collection**. They make your talk more **colourful** and bring a bit of the **world** to your words.

So, if you're **curious** about these cool phrases people use, if you want to sound a bit more **international**, or if you just love words that make you feel like you're **travelling** without moving, **Key 27** is your **guide**. It's the key to a

language adventure where you learn to say "hello" in many different ways and make your words a bit like a **global party**. Ready to open the door? Let's go! 🌍 🔑

1. **Bonjour (French):**

    - *Meaning:* Hello

    - *Pronunciation:* bon-zhoor

2. **Ciao (Italian):**

    - *Meaning:* Goodbye

    - *Pronunciation:* chow

3. **Gracias (Spanish):**

    - *Meaning:* Thank you

    - *Pronunciation:* grah-see-as

4. **Déjà vu (French):**

    - *Meaning:* Already seen; a feeling of familiarity

    - *Pronunciation:* day-zhavoo

5. **Fiesta (Spanish):**

    - *Meaning:* Party or celebration

    - *Pronunciation:* fee-es-ta

6. **Gourmet (French):**

    - *Meaning:* High-quality food

    - *Pronunciation:* goo-rmay

7. **Adieu (French):**

   - *Meaning:* Farewell
   - *Pronunciation:* ah-dyoo

8. **Ballet (French/Italian):**

   - *Meaning:* A form of dance
   - *Pronunciation:* bah-lay

9. **Feng Shui (Chinese):**

   - *Meaning:* Art of arranging spaces for harmony
   - *Pronunciation:* fungshway

10. **Gesundheit (German):**

   - *Meaning:* Bless you (after a sneeze)
   - *Pronunciation:* guh-zund-hyt

11. **Vis-à-vis (French):**

   - *Meaning:* In relation to; face to face
   - *Pronunciation:* vee-zah-vee

12. **NB (Latin - Nota Bene):**

   - *Meaning:* Note well; pay attention
   - *Pronunciation:* en-bee

13. **Rendezvous (French):**

   - *Meaning:* A meeting or gathering
   - *Pronunciation:* ron-day-voo

14. **All or Masse (French):**

- *Meaning:* All together; as a whole
- *Pronunciation:* al ohrmahs

15. **In Toto (Latin):**

- *Meaning:* In total; entirely
- *Pronunciation:* in toh-toh

16. **Faux Pas (French):**

- *Meaning:* Social blunder or mistake
- *Pronunciation:*fohpah

17. **Carpe Diem (Latin):**

- *Meaning:* Seize the day; make the most of the present moment
- *Pronunciation:*kar-pehdee-em

18. **Quid Pro Quo (Latin):**

- *Meaning:* Something given in return for something else
- *Pronunciation:*kwidprohkwoh

19. **Persona Non Grata (Latin):**

- *Meaning:* Unwelcome person
- *Pronunciation:* per-soh-nah non grah-tah

20. **Modus Operandi (Latin):**

- *Meaning:* A method of operating or functioning

- *Pronunciation:*moh-dus op-uh-ran-dee

Feel free to use this comprehensive list as a reference for both meaning and pronunciation as you explore these foreign words and phrases!

21. **Status Quo (Latin):**

    - *Meaning:* Existing state or condition

    - *Pronunciation:*stey-tuhskwoh

22. **Vice Versa (Latin):**

    - *Meaning:* The other way around

    - *Pronunciation:*vahy-suhvur-suh

23. **Per Se (Latin):**

    - *Meaning:* In itself; inherently

    - *Pronunciation:*pur say

24. **Versus (Latin):**

    - *Meaning:* Against; in contrast to

    - *Pronunciation:*vur-suhss

25. **Bona Fide (Latin):**

    - *Meaning:* Genuine; in good faith

    - *Pronunciation:* boh-nuhfahy-dee

26. **Veto (Latin):**

    - *Meaning:* Reject or prohibit

    - *Pronunciation:* vee-toh

27. **Alumni (Latin):**

- *Meaning:* Graduates (plural of alumnus/alumna)

- *Pronunciation:* uh-luhm-nahy

28. **Ad Hoc (Latin):**

- *Meaning:* For this specific purpose

- *Pronunciation:* ad hok

29. **Ex Officio (Latin):**

- *Meaning:* By virtue of one's position or status

- *Pronunciation:* eks uh-fish-ee-oh

30. **Persona Grata (Latin):**

- *Meaning:* Welcome person

- *Pronunciation:* per-soh-nah grah-tah

These phrases are often encountered in written communication and contribute to the richness and precision of language. Feel free to incorporate them into your daily writing for a touch of linguistic sophistication!

Use this space by adding to your vocabulary list:

Key 28

Common Mistakes in English

Avoiding the Mistakes Indian Speakers Make

Navigating the vast realm of the English language, **we, the non-native speakers**, often encounter a spectrum of linguistic challenges. Let's delve into some common mistakes made, acknowledging that, as non-native speakers, our journey involves embracing the language while occasionally stumbling on its intricacies.

1. **Using "According to me" instead of "In my opinion":**
   - *Explanation:* Replace "According to" with "In my opinion" or "I think" for expressing personal views, as "According to" is more suited for third-party opinions.

2. **Using "Please revert back" instead of "Please reply/respond":**
   - *Explanation:* "Revert" implies a response, making "back" redundant. Use "Please revert" or "Please reply" for clarity.

3. **Using "I am agree" instead of "I agree":**

- *Explanation:* Drop the unnecessary "am." Simply say "I agree" for grammatical correctness.

4. **Using "cope up" instead of "cope with":**

   - *Explanation:* Remove the extra "up" after "cope." The correct form is "Students must cope with stress."

5. **Using "I don't think so" instead of "I don't think (that)":**

   - *Explanation:* Insert a comma after "I don't think so" or use "I don't think (that)" for better sentence structure.

6. **Using "Although, but" instead of "Although":**

   - *Explanation:* Streamline sentences by removing the redundant "but" after "Although."

7. **Using "People cannot afford it" instead of "People can not afford it":**

   - *Explanation:* Use "cannot" without a space for proper negation.

8. **Using "I opine that (insert opinion)" instead of "I think/believe that ...", "In my opinion, ...", or "I assert that...":**

   - *Explanation:* Choose more common expressions over the formal "opine" when stating opinions.

9. **Using "Whereas" at the beginning of a sentence instead of "However":**

   - *Explanation:* Opt for "However" for a smoother transition in written discourse.

10. **Using "I am having" instead of "I have":**

- *Explanation:* For simplicity, use "I have" without the unnecessary "having."

11. **Using "Do one thing" instead of "Do this":**

- *Explanation:* For clarity, use "Do this" instead of the more informal "Do one thing."

12. **Using "Passing out" instead of "Graduating":**

- *Explanation:* Choose "Graduating" over "Passing out" to avoid confusion.

13. **Using "Prepone" instead of "Move forward":**

- *Explanation:* Use "Move forward" for clearer communication, as "Prepone" is not standard.

14. **Using "Revert back" instead of "Reply":**

- *Explanation:* Opt for "Reply" as "Revert back" is redundant.

15. **Using "Discuss about" instead of "Discuss":**

- *Explanation:* Drop "about" after "Discuss" for proper usage.

16. **Using "Out of station" instead of "Out of town":**

- *Explanation:* Use "Out of town" for a more common expression.

17. **Using "Do the needful" instead of "Do what is needed":**

- *Explanation:* Choose "Do what is needed" for clearer communication and to avoid ambiguity.

18. **Using "Kindly do the needful" instead of "Please do what is needed":**

- *Explanation:* Opt for "Please do what is needed" as a more direct and polite request.

19. **Using "I am thinking to" instead of "I am thinking of":**

- *Explanation:* Use "I am thinking of" for proper expression.

20. **Using "I am waiting for since" instead of "I have been waiting for since":**

- *Explanation:* Use the present perfect tense for ongoing actions; say "I have been waiting for since."

21. **Using "I am not having" instead of "I don't have":**

- *Explanation:* "Not having" is redundant; use "I don't have" for simplicity.

22. **Using "I am not knowing" instead of "I don't know":**

- *Explanation:* "Not knowing" is unnecessary; use "I don't know" for clarity.

23. **Using "I am not understanding" instead of "I don't understand":**

- *Explanation:* "Not understanding" is redundant; use "I don't understand" for clarity.

24. **Using "I am not having any idea" instead of "I have no idea":**

- *Explanation:* "Not having any idea" can be simplified to "I have no idea."

25. **Using "I am not having any clue" instead of "I have no clue":**

- *Explanation:* "Not having any clue" can be expressed more concisely as "I have no clue."

26. **Using "I am not having any information" instead of "I have no information":**

- *Explanation:* "Not having any information" can be simplified to "I have no information."

27. **Using "I am not having any knowledge" instead of "I have no knowledge":**

- *Explanation:* "Not having any knowledge" can be expressed more concisely as "I have no knowledge."

28. **Using "I am not having any experience" instead of "I have no experience":**

- *Explanation:* "Not having any experience" can be simplified to "I have no experience."

29. **Using "I am not having any time" instead of "I don't have time":**

- *Explanation:* "Not having any time" can be expressed more concisely as "I don't have time."

30. **Using "I am not having any money" instead of "I don't have money":**

- *Explanation:* "Not having any money" can be simplified to "I don't have money.

31. **Comprise of:**

- *Error:* Using "comprise of" instead of the correct form "comprise" or "consist of."

- *Correction:* "The team comprises experienced professionals."

32. **More better:**

- *Error:* Combining "more" with "better," which is redundant.

- *Correction:* "He performed better in the second round."

33. **Suggest me type:**

- *Error:* Incorrect usage of "suggest" followed by a direct object.

- *Correction:* "Can you suggest a type for this project?"

34. **More superior:**

- *Error:* Using "more" with "superior," which is unnecessary.

- *Correction:* "This method is superior."

35. **Discuss about:**

- *Error:* Adding "about" after "discuss," which is unnecessary.

- *Correction:* "Let's discuss the plan."

36. **Kindly revert back:**

- *Error:* Redundant use of "revert back."

- *Correction:* "Kindly revert or reply."

37. **Do one thing:**

- *Error:* Informal use; prefer a clearer instruction.

- *Correction:* "Please follow these steps."

38. **I am having:**

- *Error:* Unnecessary use of "having" after "am."

- *Correction:* "I have a meeting."

39. **Out of station:**

- *Error:* Uncommon usage; prefer "out of town."

- *Correction:* "She is currently out of town."

40. **Discuss on this topic:**

- *Error:* Using "on" after "discuss," which is redundant.
- *Correction:* "Let's discuss this topic."

41. **Different than:**

- *Error:* Using "than" instead of "from" after "different."
- *Correction:* "This approach is different from the others."

42. **Very rarely:**

- *Error:* Unnecessary use of "very" with "rarely."
- *Correction:* "He rarely visits the library."

43. **I am agree:**

- *Error:* Omitting "am" after "I."
- *Correction:* "I agree with your proposal."

44. **Cent per cent:**

- *Error:* Informal; use "100 per cent" or "cent per cent" alone.
- *Correction:* "The project is cent per cent complete."

45. **Do the needful:**

- *Error:* Formal but vague; specify the required action.
- *Correction:* "Please complete the task."

46. **Discuss about it:**

- *Error:* Omitting "about" after "discuss."

- *Correction:* "Let's discuss it."

47. **What is your good name?:**

- *Error:* Uncommon phrase; use "What is your name?"

- *Correction:* "May I know your name?"

48. **Needful things:**

- *Error:* Uncommon usage; prefer "necessary things."

- *Correction:* "Ensure you have all necessary things."

49. **Give a suggestion:**

- *Error:* Redundant use of "give"; prefer "provide" or simply "suggest."

- *Correction:* "Provide a suggestion" or "Suggest an idea."

50. **She is my own sister:**

- *Error:* Unnecessary use of "own."

- *Correction:* "She is my sister."

51. **Useful for nothing:**

- *Error:* Prefer "useless" or "not useful."

- *Correction:* "The broken pen is useless."

52. **He is my cousin brother:**

- *Error:* Unnecessary use of "brother" after "cousin."

- *Correction:* "He is my cousin."

53. He is my close friend:

- *Error:* Redundant use of "close."

- *Correction:* "He is my friend."

54. At the end of the day:

- *Error:* Overused phrase; consider alternatives.

- *Correction:* "Ultimately" or "In conclusion."

55. Undergone through:

- *Error:* Redundant use of "through" after "undergone."

- *Correction:* "I have undergone training."

57. At the earliest:

- *Error:* Overused; consider alternatives.

- *Correction:* "As soon as possible" or "Promptly."

58. He is my real brother:

- *Error:* Unnecessary use of "real."

- *Correction:* "He is my brother."

59. He is a very good person:

- *Error:* Unnecessary use of "very."

- *Correction:* "He is a good person."

60. More preferable:

- *Error:* Redundant use of "more" with "preferable."

- *Correction:* "It is preferable."

In summary, paying attention to these common mistakes can significantly improve the clarity and accuracy of written and spoken English. Whether refining expressions, avoiding redundancies, or understanding nuances, a thoughtful approach enhances language proficiency.

Less is more: Avoiding Redundant Words

In the world of words, sometimes, less is more. Redundant words, those extra bits that sneak into sentences, can quietly dull the impact of what we're saying. It's like having too many ingredients in a recipe – it just gets confusing. But when we trim down those unnecessary bits, our sentences become clear, powerful, and grab attention. It's about saying more with less, making every word count. So, let's dive into the art of saying what we mean without the extra baggage – a journey to make our words hit just right.

Let us have a list of Redundant Words:

1. **Revert back**
2. **End result**
3. **True facts**
4. **Free Gift**
5. **Past history**

6. Final outcome
7. Unexpected surprise
8. Consensus of opinion
9. Advance planning
10. Basic fundamentals
11. Future plans
12. Repeat again
13. Close proximity
14. Sum total
15. Regular routine
16. Honest truth
17. Empty space
18. Over exaggerate
19. Frozen ice
20. Advance warning
21. Join together
22. Past experience
23. Original source
24. New innovation
25. Brief summary
26. Plan ahead
27. Final conclusion
28. Absolutely essential
29. Exactly identical
30. False pretense
31. General consensus
32. First priority
33. Final verdict
34. Exact replica
35. Unexpected surprise

36. **True truth**
37. **Empty space**
38. **Join together**
39. **Plan ahead**
40. **Re-enter again**
41. **Past history**
42. **Close proximity**
43. **Future plans**
44. **Brief summary**
45. **Over exaggerate**
46. **Consensus of opinion**
47. **Advance planning**
48. **New innovation**
49. **Basic fundamentals**
50. **Final outcome**
51. **More bigger:**
52. **Reply back:**
53. **Past history:**
54. **End result:**
55. **Basic fundamentals:**
56. **Joint collaboration:**
57. **Regular routine:**
58. **New innovation:**
59. **Free gift:**
60. **Added bonus:**
61. **Past experience:**
62. **Personal belongings:**
63. **Actual facts:**
64. **Unexpected surprise:**
65. **Foreign import**

Key 29

Mind Your Tenses

(A)

Have you ever had a conversation with someone who did not use tense properly? How did you feel? Did you get what they meant? Did you correct them or ignore them? Did you laugh or get annoyed?

I remember once I talked to a friend who was learning English. He was telling me about his trip to Delhi. He said, **"I go to Delhi last month. I see Red Fort. I take selfies. I enjoy."**

I was confused by his words. I did not know if he was talking about the past or the present. I did not know if he was still in Delhi or back home. I did not know if he saw the Red Fort once or many times. I did not know if he took a selfie with the fort or something else. I did not know if he enjoyed it during the trip or after the trip.

I tried to help him by correcting his mistakes. I said, **"You mean you went to Delhi last month. You saw the Red Fort. You took a selfie. You enjoyed."**

He looked at me and said, "Yes, yes, that's what I say. **I go to Delhi last month. I see Red Fort. I take selfies. I enjoy."**

I realised that he did not understand the difference **between the past and the present tense**. He did not know how to change the form of the verbs and nouns according to the tense. He did not know how to use time words to show the time of an action or event. He did not know how to use the tense correctly.

I felt sorry for him. I wanted to help him improve his English. I wanted to teach him about tense. I wanted to show him how tense can make his speech more clear and accurate. I wanted to show him how tense can make his communication more effective and successful.

That's why I have included this piece. This lesson is not a grammar lesson that tells you all the rules of tense in a boring and complicated way. This lesson is a practical guide that helps you use words better and communicate more effectively. This knowledge will ease your spoken English journey. It will make you more confident and fluent. So, what are you waiting for? Grab this book and start learning about the tense today. You will not regret it.

Tense is one of the most important aspects of English grammar. It helps you show when an action or event happens in relation to the present time. It can also indicate the duration, completion, or repetition of an action or event. Tense can change the meaning and the mood of a sentence. It can be simple or complex, factual or hypothetical, positive or negative.

Let's get deeper into it:

1. Why Only Two Tenses?

- In English, we mainly have two tenses: **past and present.**

- Past tense uses verbs like "talked," and present tense uses verbs like "talks."

- Other tenses use helping verbs like "be" and "have," such as "was talking," "had talked," "am talking," and "have talked."

2. The Deal with Future Tenses:

- English doesn't have a special inflexion for the future.

- We express future time using "will" + the base form of the verb, like "will talk," "will be talking," etc.

- While these forms aren't technically tenses, we often call them that for convenience.

3. **Difference between Time and Tense**

   1. Time refers to the period in which an event occurs, while tense is the grammatical expression of time.

   2. Time is a concept related to our perception of reality. There are three times: past, present, and future.

   3. Tense is a grammatical category marked by verb inflexion and expresses when an

event or action happens in the flow of time.

Now, Let's Break Down Each Tense:

1. Simple Present Tense:

- Structure: Subject + Base Form of Verb

- Usage: Regular habits, general truths, unchanging situations.

- **Time Markers:** Always, usually, never, every day/week/month/year, etc.

- **Aspect Marker Words:** Seldom, rarely, hardly ever

- Example: "I always eat breakfast at 7 am."

2. Present Continuous Tense:

- Structure: Subject + To Be (am/is/are) + Present Participle (-ing)

- Usage: Actions happening now or around now.

- **Time Markers:** Now, at the moment, still, etc.

- **Aspect Marker Words:** Temporarily, briefly

- Example: "I am eating breakfast now."

3. Present Perfect Tense:

- Structure: Subject + Have/Has + Past Participle

- Usage: Actions happening before now without a specific time.

- **Time Markers:** Ever, never, already, yet, just, since, for, etc.

- **Aspect Marker Words:** Recently, so far, up to now

- Example: "I have already eaten breakfast."

4. Present Perfect Continuous Tense:

- Structure: Subject + Have/Has + Been + Present Participle (-ing)

- Usage: Actions starting in the past and continuing to now.

- **Time Markers:** For, since, how long, etc.

- **Aspect Marker Words:** Continuously, for some time

- Example: "I have been eating breakfast for 10 minutes."

5. Simple Past Tense:

- Structure: Subject + Past Simple Verb

- Usage: Completed actions in the past.

- **Time Markers:** Yesterday, last week/month/year, ago, etc.

- **Aspect Marker Words:** Once, twice, three times

- Example: "I ate breakfast an hour ago."

6. Past Continuous Tense:

- Structure: Subject + Was/Were + Present Participle (-ing)

- Usage: Ongoing actions at a specific time in the past.

- **Time Markers:** While, when, etc.

- **Aspect Marker Words:** For a while, at that time

- Example: "I was eating breakfast when you called."

7. Past Perfect Tense:

- Structure: Subject + Had + Past Participle

- Usage: Actions completed before another action in the past.

- **Time Markers:** Before, after, by the time, etc.

- **Aspect Marker Words:** Already, just, never

- Example: "I had eaten breakfast before you called."

8. Past Perfect Continuous Tense:

- Structure: Subject + Had + Been + Present Participle (-ing)

- Usage: Actions starting in the past and continuing to another point.

- **Time Markers:** For, since, etc.

- **Aspect Marker Words:** Constantly, for hours

- Example: "I had been eating breakfast for 10 minutes when you called."

9. Simple Future Tense:

- Structure: Subject + Will + Base Form of Verb

- Usage: Actions happening in the future.

- **Time Markers:** Tomorrow, next week/month/year, in a week/month/year, etc.

- **Aspect Marker Words:** Probably, certainly

- Example: "I will eat breakfast tomorrow."

10. Future Continuous Tense:

- Structure: Subject + Will + Be + Present Participle (-ing)

- Usage: Ongoing actions in the future.

- **Time Markers:** At this time tomorrow/next week, etc.

- **Aspect Marker Words:** Temporarily, for a while

- Example: "I will be eating breakfast at this time tomorrow."

11. Future Perfect Tense:

- Structure: Subject + Will + Have + Past Participle

- Usage: Actions completed before another action or time in the future.

- **Time Markers:** By, by the time, etc.

- **Aspect Marker Words:** Already, not yet

- Example: "I will have eaten breakfast by the time you arrive."

12. Future Perfect Continuous Tense:

- Structure: Subject + Will + Have + Been + Present Participle (-ing)

- Usage: Actions starting in the future and continuing up to another point.

- **Time Markers:** For, by, by the time, etc.

- **Aspect Marker Words:** Constantly, for hours

- Example: "I will have been eating breakfast for 10 minutes by the time you arrive."

Additional Tips for Easy Learning:

- **Context is Key:**

    - The tense often depends on the context of the conversation.

- **Modal Verbs:**

    - Words like "could," "would," and "will" can signal future actions.

- **Irregular Verbs:**

- Be aware of irregular verbs, which don't follow the standard "-ed" past tense ending in English.

- **Passive Voice:**

    - Tenses can also be in the passive voice, which can change the form of the verb.

Mastering tenses is like unlocking a secret code in English. Practise using these structures, pay attention to context, and soon, spotting tenses will become second nature!

Mind it: *I personally like to call it the One-Second Technique to Spotting Tenses in English. Many have benefitted from this technique.*

(B)

Sequence of Tenses

Do you want to learn how to use the sequence of tenses correctly in English? Do you want to avoid confusing your readers or listeners with inconsistent or illogical tenses? Do you want to express yourself clearly and accurately when you talk about two events happening at the same time in the past, present, or future? If you answered yes to any of these questions, then you need to pay attention to this section.

The sequence of tenses is the rule that governs the use of tenses in sentences that have more than one verb. It helps you show the relationship between the time of the main event and the time of the subordinate event. The main event is the one that is more important or central to the meaning of the sentence. The subordinate event is the one that is less important or dependent on the main event. The subordinate event is usually introduced by a subordinating conjunction, such as 'while', 'when', or 'as'.

The subordinating conjunctions 'while', 'when', and 'as' are used to connect two events that happen at the same time or in the same period of time. However, they have different meanings and uses depending on the context and the tense of the verbs. **Let's look at some examples and explanations of how to use them correctly.**

While

The conjunction 'while' is used to show that two events are happening simultaneously in the past, present, or future. It is usually followed by a verb in a continuous tense, such as the past continuous, the present continuous, or the future continuous. For example:

- She was reading a book while he was watching TV. **(past continuous + past continuous)**

- I am writing this article while you are reading it. **(present continuous + present continuous)**

- They will be studying while we will be playing. **(future continuous + future continuous)**

When

The conjunction 'when' is used to show that two events are happening at or around the same time in the past, present, or future. It can be followed by a verb in a simple tense, such as the past simple, the present simple, or the future simple, or a verb in a perfect tense, such as the past perfect, the present perfect, or the future perfect. For example:

- She called me when she arrived home. (**past simple + past simple**)

- I will call you when I finish this article. (**future simple + future simple**)

- He had already left when I got there. (**past perfect + past simple**)

As

The conjunction 'as' is used to show that two events are happening at the exact same time in the past, present, or future. It can be followed by a verb in a simple tense, such as the past simple, the present simple, or the future simple, or a verb in a continuous tense, such as the past continuous, the present continuous, or the future continuous. For example:

- As she opened the door, the phone rang. (**past simple + past simple**)

- As I am writing this article, the sun is shining. (**present continuous + present continuous**)

- As he will enter the room, the lights will go off. (**future simple + future simple**)

These are some of the basic rules and examples of how to use the sequence of tenses of two events connected by 'while', 'when', and 'as'. By following these rules, you can improve your grammar and communication skills. You can also practice by writing or speaking sentences with these conjunctions and checking your tenses. Remember, the sequence of tenses is the key to clarity and accuracy.

Here is a further guide on the topic of 'Sequence of Tenses' for new learners of English:

1. Present Simple with Future Simple When you talk about a future event that is determined by a present fact or habit, use the present simple in the main clause and the future simple in the subordinate clause. For example:

- If it **rains** tomorrow, I **will** stay at home.

2. Past Simple with Past Simple When both actions in a sentence happened in the past, use the past simple for both. For example:

- She **said** that she **wanted** to buy a car.

3. Past Simple with Past Perfect When one action happened before another action in the past, use the past simple for the later action and the past perfect for the earlier action. For example:

- She **realised** that she **had left** her purse at home.

4. Present Perfect with Past Simple When an action happened in the past but affects a present situation, use the present perfect for the present situation and the past simple for the past action. For example:

- I **have lost** my key (present situation). I **lost** it yesterday (past action).

5. Future Simple with Future Perfect When one action will be completed before another action in the future, use the future simple for the later action and the future perfect for the earlier action. For example:

- I **will go** out after I shall **have finished** my work.

Remember, understanding the sequence of tenses can greatly improve your spoken English as it allows you to express complex thoughts and situations. Keep practising.

(C)

Conditionals

Understanding Conditional Sentences: Your Path to Expressing Possibilities

*Today, let's talk about something cool—conditional sentences. Don't worry; it's not complicated. Think of it as a way to talk about **"what if" scenarios. Ready?** Let's dive in!*

1. Talking About Real Stuff with Zero Conditional

When to Use It:

- For facts that are always true.

How It Works:

- Use "if" plus a simple sentence and another simple sentence.

Examples:

1. "If the sun sets, it gets dark."

2. "If you mix red and yellow, you get orange."

What It Does:

- Helps you talk about things that are true all the time.

2. Dreaming of Possibilities with First Conditional

When to Use It:

- For things that might happen in the future.

How It Works:

- Start with "if," then use a simple sentence and add "will" and another simple sentence.

Examples:

1. "If it rains, we will stay indoors."

2. "If you study hard, you will pass the exam."

What It Does:

- Lets you talk about things that could happen.

3. Imagine the Unimaginable with a Second Conditional

When to Use It:

- For things that are not true now but could be true in the future.

How It Works:

- Start with "if," use a past simple sentence, and add "would" plus another simple sentence.

Examples:

1. "If I won the lottery, I would travel the world."

2. "If I had a pet, I would choose a dog."

What It Does:

- Helps you imagine different situations.

4. Exploring the Past with the Third Conditional

When to Use It:

- For things that didn't happen in the past, but you're imagining what might have happened if they did.

How It Works:

- Start with "if," use a past perfect sentence, and add "would have" plus a past participle.

Examples:

1. "If you had told me, I would have helped you."

2. "If they had studied, they would have passed the test."

What It Does:

- Lets you talk about unreal situations in the past.

Why You Should Care:

1. **Talk About Ideas:**

   - Use these sentences to share your thoughts and ideas with others.

2. **Tell Exciting Stories:**

   - Make your stories more interesting by talking about what could happen.

3. **Join Conversations:**

   - Feel confident joining discussions with friends or at school about future plans or dreams.

<u>Tips for Easy Learning:</u>

1. **Practice Every Day:**

   - Use these sentences when you talk or write each day.

2. **Have Fun Conversations:**

   - Talk with friends or family using these sentences in a fun way.

3. **Read Simple Stories:**

   - Read stories or watch movies with these sentences to see how they're used.

4. **Imagine Your Own Stories:**

   - Think about what you'd do in different situations. It's a fun way to practice!

Your Next Adventure:

Learning about conditional sentences is like having a superpower in English. You can express your ideas in exciting ways and join cool conversations. So, practice a bit each day, and soon you'll be a pro at talking about all kinds of possibilities. Happy learning!

Practice sheet: Correct the incorrect (bold) ones

1. After I had finished my work, **I will join** you for lunch.
2. They were walking in the park when **it starts** to rain.

3. By the time she arrives, **we would have already left** for the airport.
4. He is reading a book while his sister **watched** TV.
5. Before the storm, **they have planted** flowers in the garden.
6. **I have been studied** French for three years before I moved to Paris.
7. When the guests arrived, dinner **was already being served**.
8. The sun **will rises** again tomorrow, bringing warmth to the city.
9. By next week, **I would have completed** all my assignments.
10. While they were playing, **the cat jumps** onto the table.

Key 30

Causatives in English

You want to speak English well, right? Don't you want to express yourself clearly? Don't you want to impress your listeners?

- **I have a suggestion for you**. Why don't you learn about **causatives**? They can help you a lot with your spoken English. You can speak more fluently, confidently and accurately. You can impress more with your communication skills. ***Don't you want that?*** Then learn **causatives.** Trust me, they are very helpful.

OK, What are the Causatives then?

Causatives are verbs that show that someone or something **causes** or **influences** another person or thing to do something. For example, if you say, "I had my hair cut", you mean someone else cut your hair for you. You did not cut your hair yourself. You caused someone else to do it for you.

Causatives are very useful and common in spoken English. They can help you to:

• Avoid **long and complicated sentences**. Instead of saying, "I asked a mechanic to repair my car", you can say, **"I had my car repaired"**. This is shorter and simpler, but it has the same meaning.

- **Show your power and authority.** If you say, "I made him apologize", you show that you can force someone to do something. This can make you sound more confident and assertive.

- **Be polite and respectful.** If you say, "I got him to help me", you show that you appreciate someone's cooperation and assistance. This can make you sound more grateful and courteous.

The structure and forms of causatives depend on the type of causative verb used. English has **four common causative verbs: *have, get, make, and let*.** Each one has its meaning and structure. Here are some examples of how to use them in sentences:

- **Have:** This causative verb means to arrange for someone or something to do something. The structure **is subject + have + object + base form/past participle of the verb.** For example: **I had my hair cut. She had her car repaired. They had their house painted.**

- **Get:** This causative verb means to persuade or convince someone or something to do something. The structure is **subject + get + object + to past participle/ base/verb form.**

For example,
I got him to help me.
She got her dog to sit.
They got their children to study.

He got his hair cut.
He got his shoes mended.

- **Make:** This causative verb means to force or oblige someone or something to do something. The structure is **subject + make + object + base form of the verb.** For example, **I made him apologize. She made her students work hard. They made their guests leave.**

- **Let:** This causative verb means to allow or permit someone or something to do something. The structure is the **subject + let + object + base form of the verb. For example, I let him borrow my book. She let her cat sleep on the bed. They let their friends stay over.**

Some other Causative verbs are Cause, allow, enable, force, require, keep hold, motivate, convince, make, let.

Learning and practising causatives can improve your spoken English in many ways. You can express yourself more clearly, concisely, and correctly. You can also show your attitude and intention more effectively. Causatives can be a game changer or a practical key to mastering spoken English for beginners of English. So, what are you waiting for? Start using causatives today and see the difference!

Helpful Hints:

Sometimes, we don't do everything by ourselves. Sometimes, we ask, persuade, or force someone else to do something for us. Sometimes, we allow or help someone else to do something. To express these situations, we need to use causatives. Causatives are verbs that show who causes or influences an action to happen. Learn how to use causatives and make your spoken English more natural and accurate.

Conclusion: Elevate Your English Fluency

Congratulations on completing "30 Must Know Keys to Mastering Spoken English." This book has been meticulously crafted to guide you through a transformative journey, offering a comprehensive set of keys designed to unlock the doors to fluency.

In the pursuit of mastering spoken English, this book stands as a beacon, providing essential insights, practical strategies, and linguistic tools crucial for navigating the intricacies of spoken communication. Each key is a stepping stone, bringing you closer to the realm of fluency, where language becomes a seamless extension of your thoughts and expressions.

Whether you are a beginner seeking foundational skills or an intermediate learner striving for heightened proficiency, the collective wisdom embedded in these pages serves as a roadmap. By embracing and applying the 30 keys presented here, you embark on a holistic approach to language acquisition, fostering not only linguistic prowess but also cultural understanding and confident communication.

As you reflect on the knowledge gained within these chapters, remember that fluency is not merely about words but about the nuances, cadence, and cultural context that shape language. The journey to becoming a fluent English speaker is ongoing, and this book is a companion that empowers you to traverse that path with confidence and precision.

May the keys unveiled in this book open doors to richer conversations, meaningful connections, and a profound mastery of spoken English. Your commitment to continuous learning and improvement is the cornerstone of fluency. So, without further ado, let your linguistic journey continue, and may every spoken word be a testament to your evolving fluency.

(To Your Fluency)

Shiva